Liesel

A Century Observed

Liesel

A Century Observed

Liesel Sabloff

IngramSpark Publishing

ISBN 000-0-0000000-0-0

Cover painting: Jennifer Welty

Cover Design: Tor Anderson

Family Tree Calligraphy: Ruth Korch

Project Manager: Casey Coonerty

For more information on the fiftieth anniversary celebration of Gebrüder Becker in Chemnitz, see this article from the Jewish Museum Berlin: jmberlin.de/1933/en/07_01_congratulatory-address-marking-the-fiftieth-anniversary-of-the-gebruder-becker-glove-company-in-chemnitz.php

*This book is dedicated to all the family members on the
Becker Family and Herrmann Family Trees,
which embrace this story from beginning to end*

Two
Becker Brothers
married
Two
Mann Sisters

Eduard
Becker
m.
Lina
Mann

Karl m.
Erna
Bernstein

Lily m.
Hans
Horowitz

Arthur m.
Lotte
Frank

Adolf
Becker
m.
Flora
Mann

Grete m.
Kurt
Bernstein

Claire m.
Joseph
Muller

✳ 2ND GENERATION ESCAPED T

My Father's Family

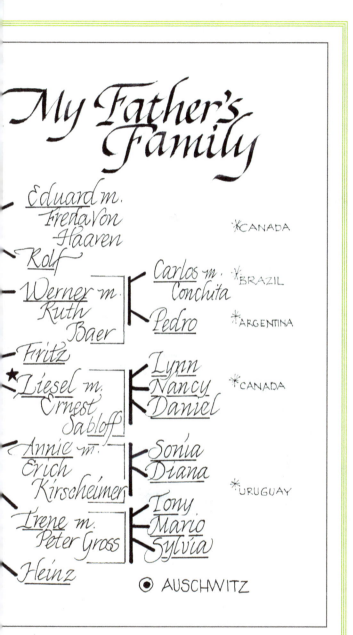

Eduard m.
Freda Von
Haaven   * CANADA

Rolf

Werner m.   Carlos m.   * BRAZIL
Ruth   Conchita
Baer   Pedro   * ARGENTINA

Fritz

* Liesel m.   Lynn   * CANADA
Ernest   Nancy
Sabloff   Daniel

Annie m.   Sonia
Erich   Diana
Kirscheimer   * URUGUAY

                 Tony
Irene m.   Mario
Peter Gross   Sylvia

Heinz   ◉ AUSCHWITZ

See pages 182-183 for Mother's Family Tree

What We Lost

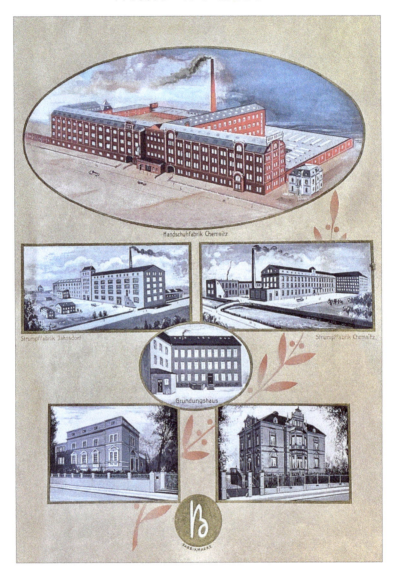

LEFT Top: *State-of-the-art Gebrüder Becker glove factory in Chemnitz, Germany, completed in 1933, fifty years after Eduard and Adolf Becker built the original factory in 1883 (oval, center page). Below the main factory are two smaller factories also owned by Gebrüder Becker. Bottom left is Karl Becker's home; bottom right is Arthur Becker's home, where many of Liesel's childhood pictures were taken.*

BELOW: *Blue Book created by employees as a gift for Arthur and Karl Becker on the fiftieth anniversary of the factory. Employees celebrated without the owners, who left for Holland due to the killing of one of their lawyers. Donated by Liesel to Jewish Museum Berlin.*

"The sheets of handmade paper inside contain a congratulatory address in elaborate calligraphy, [and] the personal signatures of forty-nine employees...[who] express their desire to have their directors back with them as soon as possible, as the "highly esteemed pioneers of the fabric glove industry." –Leonore Maier, www.jmberlin.de

L: Eduard & Adolf Becker, brothers & founders of Gebrüder Becker, built 1883 factory

R: Karl & Arthur Becker, brothers & owners in '20s, built 1933 factory

Contents

Foreword

IT IS THE YEAR 2020. In the latter part of February, it became clear that the entire world was about to experience dramatic changes in how we live and socialize with one another. Seniors, like me at ninety-four years old, were considered among the most vulnerable people to catch COVID-19. Forced to quarantine in my house alone, I decided to finally take the advice of a number of people and write my story, which I believe will shed light on a different Jewish experience than you might have read before.

I am fortunate to have been endowed with good genes. I still can take care of my house, cook for myself, and I try to exercise every day to keep my shrinking body in shape. I did inherit a substantial hearing loss from my father, but that has been corrected by state-of-the-art hearing aids that I regulate from my iPhone. That I am fairly computer literate is of significant help in these strange times.

I remain a vain woman. I colored my hair even while quarantined and hope to go to my grave well-coiffed. But until I met my husband of fifty years, no one had ever called me beautiful. I was an ordinary looking child and an ungainly teenager who became a healthy, presentable 5' 6" young adult whose interests had yet to be developed. One might call me a late bloomer, but at forty-five I finally felt fully formed.

I hope that this writing will shed light on the Jewish experience during my lifetime and serve as reminder that anti-Semitism has plagued Jews throughout the ages. This kind of hate directed at those whom people perceive as "other" is within our social fabric and seems to rise or fall as events in our world go through difficult or prosperous times. Hopefully, one day it will be a thing of the past.

Above: Eduard & Lina Becker, paternal grandparents
R: Lotte & Arthur Becker, parents

L: Arthur Becker WWI, standing right

L Top: Arthur Becker's Iron Cross announcement

R: Liesel Becker, 1931. German schoolchildren received this "Zuckertüte" (sugar cone) with school supplies

Chapter One
Leaving Germany: My Early Years

THE FIFTIETH ANNIVERSARY celebration of Gebrüder Becker, the glove factory founded by my grandfather, Eduard Becker, and his brother Adolf in 1883 in Chemnitz, Germany, was held on July 1, 1933. The current owners, my father and uncle, Arthur and Karl Becker, were not there to take part in the festivities. Their lawyer, Arthur Weiner, and two other Jewish lawyers had been brutally murdered several months before. I was seven years old.

My father had been on a selling trip in Scandinavia, Holland and Belgium, and he stayed in Holland when he learned of the murders. My mother, brother Fritz and I joined him there. He never set foot in Germany again. My uncle Karl, his wife Erna, and their two sons, Hans and Rolf also abruptly left their beautiful home in Chemnitz, right around the corner from ours, to settle in Amsterdam.

Chemnitz was my family's home for generations. My father and his siblings, Karl and Lily, were born and raised there by their loving parents, Eduard and Lina Becker. Both boys were groomed to take over the family glove and hosiery factories. (My paternal grandfather's brother Adolf married Flora, one of my paternal grandmother's four sisters.) Dad's training was interrupted by the two-year service to his country during WW I, receiving the Iron Cross. In 1920 at the age of twenty-seven, he became a full partner in Gebrüder Becker with Karl. Their beloved father and mother had passed away by then.

As a child, I loved being with my dad. To me, he was a person who radiated goodness. Although he was nobody's fool, he always dealt fairly and kindly with others. Relatives in need could always rely on him for help. He modeled how best to live one's life. My Uncle Karl was three years older than my dad and very protective of his younger brother. He was known to be a very capable administrator and served on boards of other large businesses, which made him feel quite vulnerable after the events in 1933.

My mother Lotte, a vibrant, athletic, and educated lady, was born in Leipzig in 1901 to well-established parents, Margaret and Joseph Frank. Her younger brother Rudi was her only sibling. She married my dad in 1921 and moved to Chemnitz, where they bought a

beautiful home which had a staff of three, along with a nanny for the children and a chauffeur. She was an attractive woman who had her clothes made in Berlin in the latest fashion. My parents went often to Berlin for entertainment and to

Arthur, Lotte, Fred, Liesel

visit art galleries. They acquired an ample collection of two now-famous Jewish artists, as well as other painters who are collectible today.

Chemnitz was an established industrial city. The Chemnitz River provided power to run the machines of the many factories established there in the latter part of the nineteenth century, a substantial number of which were created by Jewish industrialists who intermingled with each other for business and social reasons. They created a vibrant Jewish community centered around a beautiful conservative synagogue my dad attended regularly, wearing his top hat, the fashion at that time. I remember Dad walking through a wooded path to the factory every morning. It was his habit to come home for lunch, have a nap and return to work. He was a happy, fulfilled man.

I was accustomed to going on trips with my parents, so settling into the lovely Hotel Duin and Dale across from an animal park in the beautiful town of Bloemendaal, near Haarlem, was nothing but an adventure. Although our departure from Chemnitz was dramatic, my family was extremely fortunate. We had adequate funds in accounts in the countries in which Gebrüder Becker did business, a decision my wise Grandfather Eduard had made during the dramatic devaluation of the German mark in the 1920s. My father and uncle followed his example. For that reason, despite the adversity, great loss, and difficulties my parents had to overcome, I have lived a privileged life.

When it became clear that the German people supported Hitler and his reign would not be short lived, my parents rented a lovely home just five hundred yards from the hotel on the Lage Duin and Daalseweg, across from a large meadow where cattle roamed. My new school, *Bloemendaalse Schoolvereniging*, a progressive school that gave parents the choice of having their children streamed into a Montessori system, was just a block away; my brother attended a middle school to which he happily biked each day, like all Dutch children.

Learning Dutch was not difficult for us children; I had a small part in a play after attending school for only three months. But my father struggled to learn the language. It was fortunate, however, that the Dutch are linguists, learning French, German and then English in school, so he and Uncle Karl had no problem dealing with the lawyers and bankers they engaged to try to run Gebrüder Becker from Holland and, as the years progressed and Jews were forced from the factory, to transfer as much money out of the country as was permitted. They had to pay a large Jewish exit tax—800,000-mark *Reichsfluchtsteuer*, which equaled 25 percent of their entire worth— upon moving to Holland in 1933.

Tax levy for Jews, Nationalist Socialist era

Although they continued to exercise a certain amount of control of Gebrüder Becker as it was Aryanized, it became clear that the Nazis had threatened both their suppliers and customers not to deal with Jewish firms. It became impossible to operate and they decided to sell their assets, valued at two million marks, but they were compensated in *sperrmarks*, a devalued currency created for Jews who had emigrated. The final amount was about one-fifth the value, or about $139,000 American dollars.

The Duinhof

Fortunately, the Germans did allow crates of our belongings from the house in Chemnitz to be shipped to Holland. My parents' treasured paintings were among the items that followed us wherever we lived. Several large crates filled with furniture, carpets, lighting fixtures, china, etc. arrived in Bloemendaal. Most of those items were stored in the attic of the "Duinhof," the name of our rented property. My mother made the house into a home. Once again, she had a cook and a maid to keep our house in order. She loved the challenges of learning another language and, since she was a gregarious, outgoing woman, she took lessons and sought out volunteer organization and tennis partners to make connections with people in her new surroundings. She seemed completely happy.

But our relationship was not so easy. She found fault with how I behaved and frequently spanked me, although I cannot remember any incident that caused her to be so upset. But I do remember sitting on the stairs and crying bitter tears when my father, who had just come in the door, asked me what was wrong. After I told him what had happened, he said, "Liesel, you just have to take your mother the way she is." This wise man, who loved his wife, allowed me to feel that I had been wronged and also acknowledged that my mother's attitude toward me was unlikely to change. Although this left a mark on our mother-daughter relationship, it was so important that I had been heard by my father.

On the weekends, our home was full of other emigrant families my parents had known from their former life in Chemnitz. Among these were Jules Roos, one my father's childhood friends, and Lotte

Wedding performance

Bauman, a lifelong friend of my mother. I loved those days when I had other children to play with in my native language. We staged performances for our parents on the balcony of the house.

During the seven years we lived in Holland, I integrated fully into my wonderful Dutch environment. I made four lifelong friends who were not of my faith; Wetka, Hanneke,

Friends in Holland

Tinneke, and Lily's families opened their homes to me, and I was made to feel so very welcome. We have stayed connected our entire lives and I have returned to visit them on several occasions, once with my husband and daughter.

I have always loved playing sports and am grateful to my mother for exposing me to swimming, tennis, and riding lessons. I also took interpretive dance and piano lessons, and during our winter holidays in Switzerland, I attended a ski school and took figure

Liesel the skater

skating lessons from the same teacher as Sonja Henie, the champion of that era. In my free time I played slag ball, a form of baseball, and bicycled to the North Sea resort of Zandvoort to swim in the ocean. Even my brother used me as a goalie when he played soccer with his friends on our lawn. Throughout my teens as well as my adult life, I always felt adequately skilled in these activities to join others who invited me to participate in the sports we loved.

There were very few Jewish people living in the beautiful surroundings in which we found ourselves; I only met one Jewish girl the entire seven years we lived in Bloemendaal. I think that, had we moved to Amsterdam where there was a large Jewish community, our life in Holland would have been quite different. There was no synagogue or temple or Hebrew school in Bloemendaal, and the nearest house of worship was an ultra-orthodox Sephardic synagogue in Haarlem, twenty minutes away by bicycle. My family did attend that synagogue on High Holidays, where the women would worship in a balcony with a curtain so that no one would be distracted from their prayers. It was quite different from the service we had attended in Chemnitz in our beautiful conservative synagogue. Since there were no facilities for us children to study our history and learn to read Hebrew, my brother Fritz and I were tutored by a rabbi who came to the Duinhof. My brother celebrated his bar mitzvah in our garden in 1936. A lovely man came with his ice cream wagon to provide people with my brother's favorite treat. Visitors from Germany came to celebrate, including my maternal grandparents, Joseph and Grete Frank, cousins Claire and Josef Muller, and their son, Heinz. Of course, the Karl Becker family was present.

During the next two years, more changes took place. My kind brother, who often teasingly bossed me around, was sent to a boarding school in England. Many families who had emigrated and even those who had not yet escaped sent their sons to England. It was an expedient step to take. My cousin Hans had been in England for several years, and industrious Uncle Karl bought an interest in a glove company in that country so his son could enter the industry once he graduated from school.

Chapter Two

Exploring Our Options

IN 1937, MY PARENTS decided to take a trip to the United States, where my mother had an uncle, her father Josef's brother. Uncle Otto had emigrated from Germany many years before and lived in New York City, in a beautiful apartment on Riverside Drive. Arthur and Lotte were anxious to see America, but the main purpose of this trip was to initiate the process of obtaining visas for our family. Uncle Otto had already helped other people, but he was not able to assist my parents because the quota for German immigrants had been reached. Shamefully, the US, Canada and many other countries had closed their embassies to the desperate Jews of Europe.

Exactly when and how Dad learned of a slight opportunity for us to settle in Canada, I do not know. But not long after leaving the US, he was in touch with Mr. A.J. Paul in Montreal, who was affiliated with the Jewish Immigrant Aid Services (JIAS). He was the person who would lobby the Canadian Parliament to allow us and a few hundred others to enter Canada—at a substantial cost.

The following may come as a surprise to you. During that same year, my parents allowed me to visit my grandparents in Leipzig. It seemed that the threat in Germany had come to a momentary standstill, which made this journey possible. I accompanied a distant cousin who had visited us back to his home city of Leipzig and enjoyed spending two weeks with my witty, humorous grandfather, Joseph, and my dignified grandmother, Grete. It was the only time I ever saw the unpleasant sight of Nazis patrolling the streets. This twelve-year-old traveled back from the safety of

Holland unsupervised, with sandwiches and a nice round apple. Slicing the apple on a moving train almost caused me to lose a finger. I arrived home from this dangerous journey with my hand wrapped in gauze and a permanent scar reminding me of that trip to Leipzig in 1937.

I entered middle school that year and biked there every morning. Since the bicycle was and may still be Holland's favorite mode of transportation, everyone had to pass a test for permission to ride. In my new school, German was added to the curriculum and as I was far from a brilliant student, I was glad to have one class in which I might excel. I also played on the grass hockey team and loved that experience.

Early in 1938, many countries, including the US, Canada, and England, needed to address the numerous visa requests they were receiving from European Jews who wanted to escape the Nazi menace. To reach a unified consensus on the refugee problem, President Franklin D. Roosevelt, Prime Minister Winston Churchill, and Prime Minister Mackenzie King of Canada called for an international conference. Thirty-two countries and twenty-four volunteer organizations were invited to attend at the French resort of Evian that summer.

More than 200 international journalists also gathered at Evian to observe and report on the meetings. During the nine-day conference, delegate after delegate rose to express sympathy for the refugees. But most countries including the US, Britain, and Canada offered excuses, such as that they were already suffering because of the Great Depression and, since anti-Semitism was already widespread in their countries, more refugees would exacerbate these problems. The only country ready to receive refugees was the Dominican Republic. Thirty-two nations failed to come to any agreement about accepting Jewish refugees from the Third Reich.

Golda Meir, the future Prime Minister of Israel, attended the conference from British Mandate Palestine. She was not allowed to speak, only to observe. At a press conference she said, "There is only one thing I hope to see before I die and that is that my people should not need expressions of sympathy anymore." Hitler was jubilant. Two months after Evian, Britain and France granted Hitler the right to occupy German-speaking Sudetenland, part of Czechoslovakia, which made 120,000 Jews stateless. He then annexed Nazi-friendly Austria in May of that year. Also, during that period, the British issued a White Paper barring Jews from entering Palestine or buying land there. The Nazi regime felt emboldened by all this support.

On November 9, 1938, *Kristallnacht*—the Night of Broken Glass—was the final turning point for most European Jews. Violent anti-Jewish demonstrations broke out across Germany, Austria, and Czechoslovakia. Nazi officials depicted the riots as justified reactions to the assassination of German official Ernst vom Rath, who had been shot two days earlier by Herschel Grynszpan, a seventeen-year-old Polish Jew distraught over the deportation of his family from Germany. Over the next forty-eight hours, mobs spurred by anti-Semitic exhortations from Nazi officials destroyed synagogues—including the one in Chemnitz—plus 7,500 Jewish businesses, homes, and schools. German police and firefighters did nothing to prevent the destruction. Ninety-one Jews were murdered; 30,000 were arrested and sent to concentration camps. In addition, a fine of one billion marks, about $400 million, was imposed on the German Jewish community. This was the beginning of the Holocaust, and it prompted all Jews who had any means to depart for safe havens as quickly as possible.

My maternal grandparents came to Holland; Lily, my father's sister, and her family, the Horwitzes, went to Argentina. The Bernsteins settled in Uruguay. One of my grandmother Grete's brothers, Willi Herrmann, escaped with his family to Colombia. Distant cousins moved to Chile. Mother's dear friend and namesake, Lotte, and her daughter, Liesel, settled in England. My cousins, the Mullers, unfortunately remained in Germany.

Although the Nazis encouraged Jews to emigrate, the dangers they faced elsewhere in Europe led them to find ways to leave the continent for good. But their journeys were perilous.

In May of 1939, 937 passengers—of whom nine hundred were Jews—boarded a ship named the MS *St. Louis* headed to Cuba. The ship flew a Nazi flag but was captained by an empathetic Gustav Schroeder. Most of the passengers had purchased Cuban visas in Germany with the hope of living there while awaiting entry into the US. However, upon arriving, Cuban officials explained that their "pragmatic immigration policy" had been changed on May 5, and they refused to let most passengers disembark. All but twenty-eight had their visas revoked; twenty-two of these were Jews who had valid US visas, four were Spanish citizens, and two were Cuban nationals.

The rest of the desperate passengers formed a committee that begged the Cuban president, Manuel Sterling, and the American president, Franklin Delano Roosevelt, for sanctuary. The Cubans were indifferent, and the US was unwilling to open its doors, stating that "passengers would have to abide by the existing quota system," which meant they would be added to a waiting list. Their last hope was that Canada would allow them to land, but like the other leaders, Prime Minister Mackenzie King refused to entertain the idea.

The *St. Louis* turned around and headed back to Germany.

In my research to accurately relate this sad story, I learned that Captain Schroeder, of whom I had never heard, went to significant effort to ensure his desperate passengers a comfortable voyage across the Atlantic with fine dining, entertainment, and Shabbat services at the Friday night dinners. He assisted with their negotiations to dock in the US and Canada and even tried to run the ship aground in Miami to force the US to admit his passengers. When he had no other recourse but to turn the ship around, he made up his mind that he would not return to Germany until all his 908 passengers had been given entry to some other country. Britain, France, Holland, and Belgium complied, and he docked the *St. Louis* on June 17 in Antwerp. Later research tracing each passenger determined that 254 of those who returned to Europe were murdered during the Holocaust. After the war, Captain Schroeder was awarded the German Order of Merit and in 1993 he was named as one of the "Righteous Among the Nations" at the Yad Vashem Holocaust Museum in Israel.

When Hitler decided to occupy Poland in early 1939, the British and French governments threatened to declare war. The Germans persisted and war was declared on September 1, 1939. Holland was the next country Hitler would annex.

I was thirteen and do not recall my parents ever sharing their anxieties with me. I presume that they were very concerned about obtaining visas for Canada and it was our good fortune that, after my father and Uncle Karl each deposited $250,000 into the Royal Bank of Canada, visas for both Becker families were granted in March 1939. But my grandparents would not join us. My maternal grandmother, after hearing of friends who died at sea when their boat was torpedoed en route to the US, was too afraid.

We left almost immediately for England, where we waited approximately three weeks to board a beautiful ship, the *New Amsterdam*, to sail to New

Top: New Amsterdam to NY; L: Lotte & Arthur Becker
R: Liesel, Arthur, Lotte, & Fred en route to NY, 1939

York. It was my first time on an ocean liner, and I was not a happy sailor. It turned out that I have an inner ear problem that has existed for all my now ninety-four years.

When we arrived in New York, we checked into the Mayflower Hotel close to Columbus Circle, near my great-uncle's Riverside Drive apartment. My parents almost immediately hired an English teacher to teach us as much as possible before we left for Canada three weeks later. My brother, who was fortunate to have lived in England for several years, was already fluent. Whenever we could, the two of us would roam the beautiful, expansive Central Park across the street from the confining quarters of our hotel. We also went to the World's Fair, which held many attractions for us, but seeing the beautiful Esther Williams perform with a group of very accomplished swimmers was unforgettable.

Meeting Great-Uncle Otto, vibrant and entertaining Aunt Birdie, and their grown children was also exciting. They lived in a multilevel apartment building, something I had not seen before. This family, except for the Karl Becker family and Kurt Herrmann, a cousin of my mother's, were our only living relatives on the entire North American continent.

Otto Frank, Lotte Becker, Birdie Frank

Chapter Three
Moving to Canada

EARLY IN APRIL, eight us, our family and my Uncle Karl's family, took the train to Montreal and entered Canada as "enemy aliens," a term that was my official identity until I became a Canadian citizen and was again my designation as a resident alien in the US in the 1980s. We again settled in a hotel, the Mount Royal Hotel in the very center of downtown Montreal, on Peel Street. My room faced a well-known restaurant, Bens, which was famous for its smoked meat. I was awakened at 6:00 am every morning by the noise of people lining up to receive yesterday's bread for their daily meals. This was my first exposure to the Great Depression.

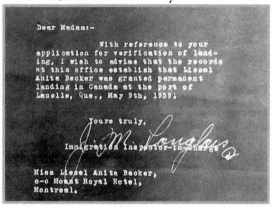

Permission to enter as resident alien

Although the end of the school year was only two-and-a-half months away, my mother marched me up to Montreal High School, four blocks from the hotel, to register me in the eighth grade. I probably spoke fewer than forty words of English. The nice teacher introduced me to the class as "Lysol" and suggested that the students help me learn English. When my mother heard that name, she felt that the name Liesel was too German sounding and that I should change my name to Betty or Anita, my middle name. My brother changed his name to Fred from the Germanic Fritz, and my cousin Hans became Edward, which was his middle name, but Liesel was my identity and I wanted to keep it. I do not recall much of my few months in that school, but I have no negative memories of that time.

What I do remember is going for my breakfast every morning to then well-known Honey Dew restaurant next to the hotel. I loved that. The staff shouted my order of two fried eggs to the kitchen when they saw me coming, and their welcoming smiles made me feel very much at home.

Still not certain whether Montreal was to be our permanent home, in June my parents decided to travel across Canada to assure themselves that this city was where we should establish ourselves. While they were away, I attended two months of summer camp, Camp Hiawatha for Jewish children. Why only Jewish children? The answer to that question circumscribed my forty-six years in Montreal.

Hiawatha was on a beautiful lake in the lovely Laurentian Mountains. There was a girls' camp on one side of the lake and a boys' camp on the other, which the now-famous Leonard Cohen attended as a boy. I slept in a bunk with five other girls, who were pleasant, but since they had known each other for years, I felt like the odd person out. Although I was never made to feel unwelcome, that feeling of being an outsider was to pervade my first eight years in Canada and resurfaced when I moved, years later, to the US.

I had English lessons in camp and believe that living in an entirely English-speaking environment helped me to learn the language more quickly. But living in a second, or for me, third language was difficult, as is well documented in Canadian book *Lost in Translation* by Polish immigrant Eva Hoffman. Suddenly my identity—as a German- and Dutch-speaking girl who had left a lifestyle and good friends behind—had to adapt to entirely different surroundings and norms, while learning another language. This was harder at thirteen or fourteen than it had been earlier; I could not communicate with the girls the way they communicated with each other, resulting in an emotional disconnect that none of us knew how to deal with.

Nonetheless, I attended Hiawatha for the next five summers, and because I was fairly accomplished at most sports, helpful, and never presented a problem, I was twice awarded the All-Around Camper Award. Although I was proud to receive it, I had the feeling that my fellow campers would really have preferred someone else, not this outsider, to have received these awards.

During my first summer at camp, Uncle Karl, my father's brother, best friend, and partner, suddenly passed away, and a month later we received the news that Dad's sister Lily had also died. These events hit my caring, family-loving father hard and he was depressed for several years. He now not only felt responsible for the welfare of his own family but also for that of his late brother; indeed, Aunt Erna and Rolf were dependent on him. Karl's older son Eduard (Edward) had already struck out on his own.

After my parents' trip across Canada, they decided we would settle in Montreal. This beautiful city on the large St. Lawrence River, flanked by Mount Royal and Westmount Mountain, was to be our home. I do not believe that they were aware of the complexities of this wonderful city and Quebec Province, which is still unique among the other Canadian provinces. Events throughout the centuries of Quebec's history have been recorded in detail, but I will offer a small window into it.

The first French settlers came to Canada in the seventeenth century and named their new home New France. During the Revolutionary wars, the English came from the south to defeat the French in Quebec in a battle on the Plains of Abraham in 1760. From that time on, the English exercised a great deal of control over the economy in Quebec. This resulted in the *Two Solitudes*, as Hugh MacLennan so aptly entitled his book describing the two segments of Quebec's population. The French-speaking population and the English lived side by side; yet their religions and their cultures were vastly different and their separate school systems contributed to maintaining these differences.

The English Canadians were entrepreneurs, predominantly Protestant, and made up approximately 40 percent of the population. The French were Catholic, and the church held great power. Their schools were run by the clergy, who did not educate their flock in the sciences or economics.

The "third solitude" of Quebec society was made up of approximately 90,000 Jews whose ancestors had escaped pogroms in Russia, Lithuania, Poland, and other East European countries during the late nineteenth and early twentieth centuries. By 1939, they had created a vibrant, successful community but were entirely socially isolated from any but commercial interaction with the other two solitudes. They built Jewish institutions—synagogues, schools, a hospital, the Young Men's Hebrew Association (YMHA), a nursing home—and organizations like the Jewish Immigration Aid Services (JIAS) that facilitated our admittance to Canada. All this was financed with private donations from the Jewish population, a new concept for German Jewish immigrants. Before the war, Germany's religious institutions had been funded by a percentage of the taxes collected, an amount determined by how many people of each religion lived in an area. Jewish immigrants now had to learn to donate to the upkeep of these institutions.

Nonetheless, anti-Semitism was rife in Quebec. The extensive sociocultural segregation of Jews in Quebec was greater than that in English Canada, the United States and even France. The French government and the Catholic church in that province made no secret of their dislike of the Jewish race.

Camp Hiawatha was my family's first association with a Jewish organization. Joining a synagogue was next. Followers of the Jewish faith have numerous choices as to how they want to worship and celebrate their religion, including Orthodox, Conservative, and Reformed denominations. We joined Temple Emanuel, a Reformed synagogue recommended by Mr. Paul. This was also where I attended and eventually graduated from Hebrew school. Uncle Karl was buried in the lovely Reformed Jewish cemetery. Temple Emanuel had an organ, families sat together at the service, and head coverings were not required. Most of the service was conducted in English with only a few Hebrew prayers. It was so very different from what my father was used to. After two years, he chose to join the beautiful conservative Shaar Hashomayim Synagogue, which reminded him of the way services had been conducted in Chemnitz. My mother accepted my father's choice. Although she worked hard for Jewish causes, she would have been content to live her life without any religious affiliation.

Hotel living was now in the past. My parents first rented a house in Westmount, a beautiful suburb of Montreal populated almost entirely by English speakers and a substantial number of Jewish families. A year later, we moved into our permanent home, also in Westmount. Aunt Erna and Rolf moved into a house only five minutes from ours. Our street, Murray Hill, was just one block long with a beautiful little park we could access by crossing one main artery. In the spring, a football/soccer field and tennis courts were available. In the winter, the little hill was readied for skiing and tobog-ganing; the tennis court became a skating

Murray Hill house

rink and the football field a hockey rink. Again, crates arrived at both our homes, this time from Holland. It was comforting to have our homes furnished with familiar items, including the treasured paintings. The one thing I missed, though, was my bicycle. My parents felt the terrain in Montreal was too hilly and therefore dangerous.

Jewish students were tolerated in the Protestant school system, and I became a student at Westmount High School. To this day I do not know who decided that I should be registered in a program that, upon graduation, rewarded me with a high school leaving certificate instead of the matriculation certificate that was required to be accepted in any of the universities. My parents or the principal or both decided that the less-demanding program would be easier for me to handle as I was adapting to my new surroundings and becoming proficient in English.

Throughout the next years, our social interactions were entirely with other immigrants. "Birds of a feather flock together." The families that became our close friends all had entered Canada on special visas. The Carl Cahn family were sponsored by the Protestant Birks family, who owned the largest jewelry chain in Canada and had dealt with Mary Cahn's family in the same line of business in Mainz. The Cahn's eldest son was the first Jew ever to be employed in their stores. Many businesses, including banks and insurance companies, did not employ Jews.

Jules Roos, my father's friend, had also moved to Montreal from Amsterdam with his wife Minnie and their four children. Their orphaned niece joined their family and Rena became one of my closest friends, which she still is at ninety-six. Another family was admitted because they were experts in the plywood industry and had the money to establish and run a factory, a company that still exists today and is run by their grandson, Robert Hirscheimer. Robert's grandparents were my parents' good friends; his parents, Ernie and Rita, became my lifelong friends.

Arthur & Lotte Beckman's 25th anniversary, all immigrants; Liesel far right

The Hirscheimers were one of ten immigrant couples of my parents' generation who became a close-knit group. For years, we, their children, felt more at ease with one another than we did with our cohorts who were born Jewish Canadians. This was, in part, because the established Jewish community of mostly Eastern European descent was not welcoming to German Jewish immigrants. Even as a teenager I could feel their antipathy.

When I discussed this with my wise father, he affirmed my feelings and explained that German Jews had looked down upon Eastern European Jews for decades. My father explained that Rabbi Moses Mendelssohn (b.1729, d.1786) bore some responsibility for this. Through his advocacy of religious tolerance and the prestige of his own intellectual accomplishments, he did much to further the emancipation of the Jews from prevailing social, cultural, political, and economic restrictions in Germany, which gave them a feeling of superiority. The established Jewish community, in turn, now showed their antipathy to us, and some even went as far as to accuse us of not helping our German Jewish family and friends escape the Nazi menace.

How easily hate and envy can be aroused. Will we ever learn?

As we settled in Montreal, the war in Europe raged. Holland was annexed in September 1940 and my grandparents found themselves stranded in an extremely dangerous situation. They were not able to communicate with us as Canada was deemed an enemy nation. My grandmother was able to send Red Cross notes of twenty-five words to her brother in Cali, Colombia, which he forwarded to us. They are in my possession today.

While my family was learning to adapt to their new surroundings, Germany added another insult to the injuries already inflicted. In 1941, they published a list of all German Jews, stripping them of their German citizenship. For every male, "Israel" was attached to their given name, and to every woman's name they added "Sarah," another example of the cruelty of Hitler's regime.

Fortunately, time is a great healer and my father's depression was now under control. He and his longtime trusted friend decided

Karl, Erna, Hans & Rolf Becker (underlined) in loss of citizenship rolls; note addition of "Israel" & "Sarah'" to names

to go into business together. Belgium Glove & Hosiery, a chain store operation that sold ladies' wear, was up for sale. After a thorough investigation of the organization's health, Dad joined Jules Roos and a Canadian partner, Philip Cohen, to buy the company.

This investment not only gave my father the opportunity to use his expertise as a glove and hosiery manufacturer but also allowed my brother to become involved in the business after years of working in an accountant's office. Fred began to work at Belgium Glove and gave it his all, but working under three strong bosses proved too difficult for him. After several years, he moved to Toronto where he found work in the toy industry, and Toronto became his permanent home.

As she had been in Holland, my mother became a diligent, devoted volunteer in organizations such as the Jewish Immigrant Aid Services of Canada (JIAS), spending a great deal of her time in the effort to help hundreds of German Jewish men who, like my brother and cousin, been sent as boys to study in England.

As Germans, these young men were considered enemy aliens—it did not matter to the government that they were Jewish. More than 7,000 of these men were imprisoned in England in 1941 as enemy aliens and sent to Canada as well as to Australia with German prisoners of war, where they were forced to live in prisons with their enemies. A group of 2,300 men lived in such an environment in Saint John, New Brunswick, 150 miles from Montreal. When the authorities realized this was an untenable situation, they separated the Jews from the Nazi groups. Now the young Jewish men were forced to wear tee shirts with a red dot about ten inches in diameter imprinted on their backs as their new identity. They had to perform exhausting manual labor and their nutrition was inadequate.

But they had each other. They formed study groups, played music, and managed to survive this most unbelievable situation. After approximately two years of imprisonment, a window of opportunity opened for those who could be sponsored by members of the Montreal Jewish community either to continue their education or work in one of the members' businesses. My parents sponsored a student of mathematics, Jim (Joachim) Lambeck, who was to become an eminent professor at McGill University. My dad also hired Otto Hirschfeld to work in his firm. Otto became a treasured employee as well as a good friend to our entire family. My mother and the dedicated group she worked with found sponsors for many of these young men, who were to make their mark in Canada. Their stories that have been well documented in the book *Deemed Suspect* by the one of these men, Eric Koch.

There were many Sunday afternoons when fifteen or twenty of these former detainees would gather in our home, which offered them a place to be together and share their new experiences. I also enjoyed being among these interesting and accomplished young men who had lived imprisoned for years.

Would I ever have a picture of my wedding like my parents' in 1921?

*Liesel's parents' wedding in Germany: Lotte Frank Becker & Arthur Becker standing, center
L to R: Erna & Karl Becker, Liesel Goldschmidt, Grete Frank, Rudi Frank, Josef Frank,
and Uerner, Hans and Lily Horowitz*

Chapter Four
Growing Up and Into My Life

HOW TO BEST DESCRIBE my development during these formative years? At home, I heard my mother's praise for others' accomplishments, but the first time I recall her saying something nice about me was when I was sixty-five, visiting her in Florida. It was her nature to proclaim that things were either horrible or wonderful, whether it was a bus ride or something someone did or said. She loved to tell stories of her experiences, believing them to be of great interest to others. My life was so dull compared to hers. I tried to keep myself out of her spotlight. I was not a great student and was awkward in adapting to my surroundings. I lived as if behind an imaginary fence that only my immigrant cohorts and a few new friends could easily cross, but that kept me from others whose inner circles I was afraid to enter. My education zigzagged over the years because neither my parents or I understood how the Canadian educational system worked, nor the consequences of the discriminatory measures that were in place.

The Canadian Jewish historian Irving Arbella describes Canada during the 1920s and 1930s as "a benighted, xenophobic, anti-Semitic country" in which Jews were excluded from almost every sector of society. Virtually every Canadian university that had a sizable Jewish population implemented discriminatory measures. In 1913, 6.8 percent of McGill University students were Jewish; by 1924, this had risen to 25 percent. According to Ira Robinson, Professor of Jewish Studies at Montreal's Concordia University, Jewish students were perceived as too "academically concentrated" compared to those who were more "well-rounded." These were code words to legitimize the reduction of Jewish students at McGill, policies that were "purely administrative" and never made official. By 1935, the proportion of McGill's Jewish students had dropped to 12 percent.

If I intended to further my education, I had to upgrade my high school certificate by taking courses in algebra and geometry, which I did the year after graduation. I also took a business course to cover all my bases, learning shorthand and typing. I did well enough to enter Macdonald College, an affiliated college of McGill University, twenty-five miles outside of Montreal. Of the three faculties it offered—Household Science, Teaching and Agriculture—I chose the last. I loved the outdoors and had such good memories of the peaceful meadow where cows grazed in front of our house in Holland. My father also liked my choice and had visions of buying a farm for his daughter when she graduated.

As it turned out, I was now in a faculty with approximately thirty young men and one other young woman, a farmer's daughter. Yes, we learned about crop rotation, breeding different breeds of cattle, fertilization and much, much more, but agricultural engineering was not what I had in mind. My academic courses were trigonometry, calculus, physics, zoology, organic and inorganic chemistry. Math and science were not my forte. Despite waning interest in my studies, I did enjoy the two years I lived on the campus with young people on the move, some from faraway countries. That was an education in itself. I can still hear one girl singing daily on her way to the shower, "Oh, what a beautiful morning…" No one could stop her expression of joy at being alive. I made friends, attended the socials, and had the good fortune to have a lovely roommate named Joya who came from Haiti to become a teacher. We stayed connected for many years.

Studying agriculture required me to work on farms during the summer months, the best months of my two years at college. My parents had immigrant friends who owned a farm in northern Ontario where I spent the first summer. I loved living with the family and taking part in all the chores that needed to be done.

The experience of watching ten little piglets appearing one after another, breaking the birth sac and finding the sow's teats, was a revelation. Helping to pull a calf from the cow during a breech birth was exciting as well as educational. When our second daughter was born, I had a similar experience.

The next summer, I wanted to work on a dairy farm. How does one find a Jewish dairy farmer? You contact the Jewish agricultural agency in New York. I chose a farm in Connecticut off a highway between Lebanon and Willimantic, an area I later learned that was home to numerous Jewish farmers who, like my family, were immigrants from Eastern Europe and had been assisted by JIAS as early as 1910.

The owners and their strapping son, Eugene, who was a little older than I, made me feel most welcome. The young man became my mentor not only on the farm but also at the local social hall, where I learned to square dance. I rose at 5:00 am every morning to milk the cows by hand, not such an easy exercise with tails swinging and legs kicking if the pressure of my hands was not to their liking. I persevered, however, and was then permitted to use the milking machines. I also became an expert at shoveling manure. My animal husbandry

Liesel at work on the farm

course at Macdonald had prepared me to recognize which cows are good breeders and how one judges the structure of the udders to determine the potential strength of their milk production. It was interesting to see these criteria applied in this successful farm.

My mentor was a sweet and caring young man who began to show he cared for me. I had all the desires of a twenty-year-old woman but minimal experience with male companions. However, I did know that Eugene could not be my choice of husband. He was less sophisticated than the people I knew, and I was unprepared to respond to his sexual advances.

It was now August 1946. World War II was over; the Allies had won. We learned that my maternal grandmother, Margarete Frank, did not survive; but it was not until 1988 that I learned she died in Auschwitz and received detailed information of her transport to that camp. During the war, we had no concrete knowledge of what was going on. If my parents knew what was happening, they kept it from me. On an Elderhostel trip to Eastern Europe in 2005, which included a visit to Auschwitz, I shared all the information about her life with my fellow travelers. It was at that time that she would have her memorial.

We focused on and celebrated the good things in life, such as my parents' twenty-fifth anniversary on August 22, 1946. When I look at pictures of those who attended that weekend celebration in Lake Placid, I see only immigrants. Although we had gotten our Canadian citizenship, we were still an isolated group, most at ease with each other. This was about to change when I returned to Montreal and received the most important phone call of my life.

On August 30, I heard the confident voice of my future husband for the first time. Ernie Sabloff explained that a mutual good friend had given him my name and he asked if I would be interested to go out with him the following evening. I was intrigued and said yes. The next evening a very handsome, well-built man picked me up and politely led me to his ancient car which, he claimed, was more likely to start on a hill. Luckily, I lived on a great one. We

Ernie Sabloff

went to a nightclub and although it was not the easiest venue to have a conversation, I did learn that I was in the company of a charming, mature Jewish man who, after having received his BSC from McGill University, had enlisted in the army to fight the Nazi menace. He went overseas as a lieutenant in 1941 with a specialty in air support. I also learned that I was last on a list of eleven girls our friend had given him, and I assumed he had dated all of them and then had nowhere else to go—a good story that I tell people who ask me how I met Ernie. I did believe that we both enjoyed the evening, but I really had no inkling if I was ever going to hear from this incredibly attractive man again.

The next day I found out that I had passed the preliminary test and was about to pass another when Ernie called to ask me to go sailing with him. He rented a boat on the mighty St. Lawrence, which was calm that Sunday morning. He proved to be an avid and experienced sailor—and I was not. Our ocean crossing had taught me to avoid turbulent waters. After a short time, the winds started to blow, the water became rough, and I requested to be returned to shore, where I told him that I would happily await his return if he wanted to take advantage of the great sailing weather.

"Really?" he asked, appreciating my understanding, and he did.

No relationship moves in straight line, but I began to hope that I had met the man who might become my husband. Yet, throughout the next month, I only heard from Ernie sporadically and was plagued by doubt. I learned that he was still seeing a lovely blonde girl he had dated before entering the service. Had he really needed the list of the eleven potential "old maids?" Today, in 2020, that last statement sounds bizarre, but post-WW II, when there was not an abundance of available young men and most women were not adequately educated to be self-sufficient, young people were expected to be married in their early twenties.

Happily, by November I began to see Ernie more frequently. My parents did what responsible parents did; they contacted people in the community who knew him, and his family, to assure themselves that I was dating an upstanding Jewish citizen. My father also invited Ernie to go on a two-day fishing trip to get to know him better. He passed those tests with flying colors. I have been asked whether I fell head-over-heels in love with this man. My thoughtful response was no. I was enormously attracted to him but kept a check on my emotions for fear of being disappointed.

My confidence in myself was fragile. Was I lovable? Why were my hips so wide and my legs not elegant and long? My hair was thick and wavy, but I would have loved to have silky long hair. My education was incomplete. My mother was no help when she said,

"That Ernie is too handsome." Was there a doubt in her mind that her daughter would be able to satisfy all his needs? It became clear that Ernie saw a different Liesel than the image I had of myself. Yet, he was in no position to ask anyone to marry him, as his aim was to get a law degree while taking advantage of the GI Bill that offered veterans the ability to go back to university with $80 a month to cover living expenses. But both of our parents were delighted with our love for each other and wanted to see us married. They decided to help us get established; we would supplement our small income with my work in a chemical lab and Ernie's job for a debt-collecting agency. We were engaged in February and would have preferred my mother to plan a small wedding, but that was not to be. Three hundred people were present at our nuptials on May 22, 1947.

Before the wedding, all the members of my future family gathered at the home of Ernie's parents, Hymie and Ethel Sabloff, to welcome me and my family. Ernie's grandmother Bubby, whom I learned to love and admire, his brothers Murray and Bob, two aunts, an uncle, and Cousin Eric lined up to shower me and my family with hugs and kisses. Their warmth and affection were overwhelming and welcoming, and vastly different from my reserved upbringing.

Ernie's extended family were all immigrants who had escaped from Czarist Russia in the early years of the twentieth century. My father-in-law Hymie had left Russia at the age of thirteen to avoid being forced to enlist in the Czarist army for twenty-five years. When he arrived in Montreal early in the twentieth century, distant cousins welcomed him. He worked hard to pay for two of his sisters to join him, and they all became upstanding citizens and assets to the Canadian nation.

Bubby was Ethel's mother, and her story can be likened to that of Fiddler on the Roof. She and her husband left Russia, fearing the violent pogroms in their neighborhood. Their four children, of which Ethel was the eldest, were born in Canada. Unfortunately, Bubby's husband died during the outbreak of the Spanish flu in 1918 and she became her family's sole breadwinner.

Ernie adored his mother. With all his exuberance and love, I watched him lift her off her feet and place her on a tall dresser, like a throne. Throughout my marriage, I never knew when this affectionate man would pick me up to show his joy of seeing me—and I was no lightweight. It could be at home or in the middle of a busy shopping center! Becoming part of the Sabloff family changed my life enormously. I finally began to feel accepted in this Third Solitude of Quebec, and slowly began to understand that I could participate fully in the life of the community.

We were married in the beautiful synagogue to which both our parents belonged by Rabbi Shuchat, a contemporary of ours. In his speech he claimed that he was uniting the best of two continents. We now had to try to live up to that.

Above: Ernie & Liesel; Below: Wedding party, Bubby second from left

Daniel, Ernie, Lynn, Liesel, Nancy, 1955

Chapter Five
Early Married Life

ERNIE LOVED PLANNING trips and had a well-planned schedule written out for our honeymoon. Washington was our cultural experience; in Virginia Beach we relaxed; and we rounded it off with a visit to good friends in Boston. In those days, he had to assure himself that the hotels we stayed in welcomed Jews. Many hotels, beaches, and clubs in Quebec, and some in the rest of Canada as well as the US, posted signs outside of their establishments saying "Restricted," or more explicitly, "No Dogs or Jews Allowed."

In 1947, Hollywood, which was controlled to a large extent by Jewish producers, decided to make a movie entitled *Gentleman's Agreement*, starring Gregory Peck, to expose these discriminations as a norm in the US.

Our honeymoon was the first of the well-researched and interesting trips we took to Italy, France, Austria, Spain, Portugal, Morocco, and England during our fifty years together. We also visited the State of Israel together five times, when it became possible.

When we returned to our well-appointed apartment, it suddenly dawned on me that I had no knowledge of how to prepare a meal. My mother had never cooked anything but a cherry-pineapple tart and all I knew was how to prepare eggs. I had been given *The Boston Cookbook* and *The Joy of Cooking*, recommended cookbooks of that era, but had barely opened them. To make matters worse, our Bubby, who kept a strictly kosher household, had the kosher butcher deliver a chicken wrapped in newspaper to our apartment on the first Friday morning we were home. Picture me unwrapping the parcel and finding a whole bird with its neck still attached, feathers yet to be removed and unformed eggs still inside its carcass. Nearly all the occupants in this completely new apartment building were Jewish, and I had the good fortune to have an experienced cook as a neighbor. I easily accessed Sylvia's back door from mine, and she became my cooking mentor. She also kept a kosher household.

"Not kosher" (meaning "it's not okay") is now commonly used in the English language, but the Bible specifically uses *kosher* to describe how Jews are to conduct themselves in preparing meals; it also defines what foods are permissible and which should not be eaten at the same time, such as dairy products and meat. Through the ages, these laws became even more refined and complex. Now a kosher household might have three sets of dishes and cutlery—one for meat, one for dairy and one just for Passover—and two dishwashers. Of course, just as in other religions, prayers of thanks are recited at every meal.

Was it now expected of me to make my household kosher so that others who adhered to the laws of *kashrut* could come to our home for dinner? My family of emancipated German Jews never kept a kosher household in Germany or in Canada, and Ernie and I agreed to not make our home kosher. The majority of the Eastern European Jews in Canada did keep kosher homes to affirm their affiliation to their Jewish heritage, yet many disregarded kosher rules when eating out in restaurants. This dichotomy was difficult for me to understand but began to make sense when I learned the following from a wonderful orthodox rabbi much later in my life. He claimed that all forms of Judaism are acceptable to our G-d. Even I, who cannot believe in a G-d who allowed the Holocaust to happen, and whom I cannot see or hear, would be a valuable member of the Jewish tradition if I did His work on earth and followed the Golden Rule by treating others as I wished to be treated.

In 1948, the Montreal Jewish community celebrated the creation of Israel, the first Jewish state. How could any Jewish person not be joyous, knowing there was a place to escape to if anti-Semitism anywhere made their life unbearable? The Law of Return of 1950 guaranteed that right to all who could prove their Jewish ancestry.

Between 1948–1951, 700,000 Jews from every continent moved to Israel, leaving $150 billion in goods and property behind. Over the following decades, Israel's Ministries of Absorption, Labor, and Education devised programs to integrate all who came from various cultures into Israeli society, so they could learn to live and work in harmony and create a viable and secure nation.

My life with Ernie was serene. He had begun law school at McGill in September 1947 and his law studies assumed most of his time. He loved to have me sit nearby while he absorbed the law of the land and made me his interlocutor. I learned how to question him on what he was studying and so gained a bit of knowledge about the laws of our large country. In Quebec, civil law was based on the Napoleonic Code, an historic practice from the seventeenth century when Quebec was known as New France. Common law based on the British legal system was practiced in the rest of Canada, and the entire nation followed the Criminal Code. McGill University law students were examined on all three codes, but then had to choose whether to take the bar exam to become lawyers or to practice the notarial profession, which excluded all litigation law. Even before he started his studies, Ernie had decided that he wanted to be a notary. He took the Notarial Board exam in 1949 and went to work for a notary the following year.

My husband was also a gifted sculptor. He did not know this until he had his handwriting read at a party by an accredited handwriting expert, who also saw a competent lawyer in his script. My father was not surprised that handwriting analysis is extremely revealing. He told us that all employees of Gebrüder Becker were asked to write a letter of application in their own writing, which an expert then interpreted, revealing the competence of the applicant. I promptly bought some books on the subject.

We planned to have our first child after Ernie graduated, but life had other ideas, and by the summer of 1948 I was pregnant with our daughter Lynn. My undemanding husband had expressed only one wish when we got married: "Don't ever become a fat lady."

While pregnant I turned into a blimp; I gained sixty pounds. Ernie never said a word.

Unlike today, where hospitals make courses available for new parents to prepare for their momentous event, we only had books by Dr. Spock and Dr. Arnold Gesell to tell us what was in store for us. I cannot even remember getting one word of advice from either my mother or my mother-in-law. I had never held a baby in my arms. My labor pains started on February 1, 1949. I immediately went to the hospital and was told that they did not know when Lynn would decide to leave my womb; Ernie should go home and would be called when she arrived. I was beside myself. I wanted him to stay, but it was not until 1960 that a man could stay in the room with his wife until she was ready to give birth. By the 1970s, men could be present and even lovingly hold their wives during the birth.

Fortunately, our beautiful, healthy little girl arrived on February 2nd. We spent another nine days in the hospital. As all parents know, the miracle of giving birth to a child is life changing. Being there for the needs of this little innocent being proved to be so important, sometimes frightening, and yet so very rewarding.

4 generations: Ethel, Bubby, Lynn, Liesel

Lynn needed siblings and we loved having a baby around, so two-and-a-half years later our Nancy was born, and three years after that Daniel appeared on the scene. These three little people's personalities were so different. Lynn began to wave her hands and insist on doing things "by myself" at an early age. She loved to play with her imaginary friends under the dining table. Nancy was the cuddliest child who enjoyed performing. At eighteen months, she imitated Marilyn Monroe and sang "Freres Jacques." Daniel was our bright, active, compliant ball-playing boy. No cops and robbers for him.

During these childbearing years, their proud dad graduated from law school and successfully passed the Notarial Board exam. Ernest Sabloff, Notary Public, had completed several registered deeds for clients; these deeds would total more than 26,000 over the course of his entire career. Our little family always knew when Daddy was approaching home. He would either whistle or sing the song I had heard at college and taught him upon

Nancy, Daniel, Lynn

our marriage: "…and in my future life she is going to be my happy wife. How the heck did you find that out? She told me so…"

Those were also peaceful years for my parents. They were proud grandparents and enjoyed seeing our family every Friday night to celebrate the beginning of Shabbat at their home or at Aunt Erna's house. It became a tradition that we all looked forward to. Although my Aunt Erna, an obsessive housekeeper, found it hard to cope with my children's often sticky fingers leaving dirty marks on her towels, she was such a good person. Yet she made life so difficult for herself and those around her. She was extremely fortunate to have my father's help in looking after her affairs. In the early '50s, Dad became aware that although dispossessed Jews from East Germany could not claim their property, the West German government was now paying pensions to those who escaped. The amounts were prorated according to the position you held upon departure. Aunt Erna and each of my parents received approximately $10,000 annually from Germany for the rest of their lives.

At the same time, Dad told me that I needed to go to the German Consulate to claim $1,000 for the interruption of my education. He said they wanted me to relate my sorry tale to them. At first I was stunned, but on reflection, I realized that I was deserving of this gift and might even use it to eventually further my education. They agreed, and I received $1,000.

In 1954, when I was pregnant with Daniel, my parents decided it was time for them to downsize. They moved their prize possessions to a large duplex and offered 638 Murray Hill, including some furniture and a few paintings, to Ernie and me for a minimal sum. We were thrilled. I loved the house and the location, including the fact that it was near a great public school that our children could walk to in five minutes.

But life, as all mortals know, does have its dark moments.

Ernie's beloved mother Ethel died instantly when an aneurism suddenly burst while visiting with her mother, Bubby, and her two sisters. Of course, we were all devasted to lose this lovely lady who was only fifty-four. My father-in-law was in shock and for many months could not imagine his life without her. Unfortunately, our Bubby was also to lose her youngest child, Uncle Mort, to a heart attack three days later. This was not the normal order of things. This eighty-year-old never expected to survive her children. The only reason she still wanted to live was to see her great-grandchildren grow and to welcome any babies yet to be born. My brother-in-law Bob was now married to my bright and extremely mature sister-in-law, Ellen, and they obliged. Their little ones restored Bubby with the will to live.

My little family played out its own drama in the winter of 1956. Ernie, weakened by an operation, went with the three children and me to Murray Park to go sledding and our accident-prone, five-year-old Nancy slid into a big, dangerously positioned tree. She was bleeding from an ear and had to be hospitalized. The prognosis did not sound encouraging. Then Daniel promptly fell, splitting his lip so badly that we suspected the repair would not restore his beautiful little lips. Thankfully, Nancy did not sustain permanent damage, Daniel's lips were restored to perfection, and the anxious father regained his usual good health.

But these events and the news that my cousin Rolf had committed suicide seemed just too much for my nervous system. Despite my awareness of all my good fortune, I found myself in a deep depression for the next six months. Only others who have gone through this will understand the sadness and despair at not being able to function rationally. I could not absorb anything I read and even prayed to a G-d that I never believed could hear me. Doctors prescribed pills that did not alleviate my condition. Finally, I was sent to a psychiatrist who unknowingly cured me by making me so incredibly angry.

On my second visit to this "great" man, I was excited because while sitting in the waiting room I had found myself, after so many months of not being able to concentrate, reading and absorbing an article about the wild horse preserve in Eastern Canada. I could not wait to tell the doctor about this breakthrough. He listened to my tale, asked me to lie down on the couch and then thoughtfully responded that, of course, what I had been reading related to my sex life with my husband.

I left the office in anger and amazement, feeling that he had missed the point entirely. As I drove toward my home, I recall tears streaming down my face while screaming that only myself could help me to deal with this condition. As a compliant person who grew up unable to contradict my parents and who did not easily express anger, feeling this depth of emotion was new.

Throughout my entire life, with its ups and downs, this was my one and only depression. From it I learned to have empathy for others who suffer from this condition, in many cases far more severe than mine.

L: Edgar & Ruth Cohen;
friends & fellow travelers;
Below: Bernie & Ruth Issenman

Chapter Six

At Home and Abroad

OUR FAMILY HAD NOW integrated into the tightly knit Jewish community in which we lived. My father was respected as a capable, honorable businessman and a contributor to Jewish causes, and my mother was admired and respected for her devotion to numerous volunteer organizations and her interest in the arts and music. They became members of Elm Ridge, the Jewish golf club, and made friends with those who had earlier rejected them as undesirable German Jews. I, who for the past fifteen years in Canada had felt like an outsider, was now very much at home with the friends Ernie and I had made. Many of them were couples who had lived the immigrant experience and my worldly husband enjoyed being among them.

We joined a Bible study group led by Rabbi Shuchat, who had married us. Our textbook was the Joseph Herman Hertz commentary and we learned how to interpret each phrase of that great book. We spent years in monthly meetings during which we became close friends with Ruth and Edgar Cohen (a cousin of the famous Leonard Cohen) and Ruth and Bernie Issenman, with whom we would travel. Eventually, we followed the Issenmans to California when trouble erupted in Quebec. Ernie also joined a chapter of B'nai B'rith, "Children of the Covenant," the oldest Jewish service organization in the world, committed to the security and continuity of the Jewish people and the State of Israel. It is active in combating anti-Semitism and bigotry, and for human rights. When he served as president of his chapter, they won an award for setting up an extraordinarily successful swimming program for handicapped children.

Now that our two girls were going to school and Daniel was well cared for by Betty, our help, I, like most women of that era who lived in great comfort, had the time to follow in my mother's footsteps and become a volunteer. I supported Jewish organizations but never enjoyed the fundraising or committee meetings one had to participate in to become an asset to the organization. I derived greater satisfaction by helping individuals, and over the course of the next fifteen years trained to volunteer my time working with psychiatric patients at the Jewish Hospital. I worked with parents of severely autistic children at the Montreal Children's Hospital, taught a special reading program in an inner-city school, and eventually worked at the Hope and Cope cancer program at Jewish General.

But these activities did not take up all my free time. I skied in the Laurentians when the snow was perfect and played tennis in warmer weather. It also seemed important to broaden my horizons. With my dear friend Rita Hirscheimer, I attended classes at Concordia University that were of interest to both of us. History intrigued us more than anything else. We studied African, Chinese, and European history and much later, when we needed a better understanding of the history of Quebec, we attended a course on that subject. We also tried hard to improve our French and gained a greater understanding of Quebec culture by joining a group led by a charming young Quebecois man with whom we attended French-Canadian theater performances and then discussed, in our broken French, what we had seen.

Throughout the '50s we escaped the heat by spending two months at our family cottage in the Laurentians along with other Jewish families, where our children learned to swim and sail with their dad in his "sunfish," his sailboat. In the winter, we rented a cottage near a skiing facility with the Cohens and their three children and skied as a family. Learning more about cooking from Ruth was a bonus. I still make her famous apple pie.

In 1959 we received an invitation from someone Ernie greatly admired to spend a weekend at Northwick Park in Gloucestershire, England. Captain George Spencer Churchill, a cousin of Winston's, welcomed WW II soldiers to spend their leaves at his estate. He also allowed a field hospital to be built on his property which, at the end of the war, became the largest Polish refugee camp in the country from 1946–1965.

My husband had had the good fortune to spend several of his leaves at Northwick in the captain's company. Captain Churchill had fought in the Boer War from 1899–1902 and understood the need for active service men to have downtime when on leave. But there was much more to be learned from this intelligent and knowledgeable gentleman. Having inherited the estate from his aunt, with a house that had its origins in the fourteenth century and an art collection that spanned thousands of years, he decided to expand this collection by seeking out art that needed to be rescued and restored to its former beauty.

Churchill was extremely successful in this endeavor. In an art book entitled *Great Private Collections* depicting examples of his treasures, it is mentioned that he was the least selfish of collectors and that it is seldom that some pictures or objects are not on loan to exhibitions in various parts of the world. How could we forego this opportunity to have Ernie take me to this great estate and meet this interesting man? The captain had developed a fondness for the young Canadian he hosted during the war and to whom he had taught the game of squash, which had become my husband's favorite way to exercise.

Ernie had never described the property to me, so I did not know what to expect. As we approached, whenever we passed a large property, I asked if this was it. When we finally drove up to the grand house, I was overwhelmed—and this was the back entrance, where the butler welcomed us, took our luggage, and informed us that Captain would see us at teatime. He led us through the back door of the very cold house to our enormous cold bedroom with what seemed an even larger bathroom. He then suggested that we might want to take a walk before tea. We did that and when we returned to the room, I found that our luggage had been unpacked and placed into the beautiful armoire. How surprising and embarrassing!

The butler returned to lead us to a ridiculously small room with a roaring fire ablaze and a good-looking, reserved, eighty-year-old British gentleman who greeted us warmly. We drank tea from very delicate porcelain teacups and ate the accompanying crumpets while Captain questioned Ernie about his profession and our family life.

At our request, he led us through his art gallery. His reserve disappeared as we viewed his collection, housed in a well-built structure as big as a large barn. Three rows of paintings covered the walls, and long tables on the floor were covered with sculptures and precious artifacts. He talked enthusiastically of his excitement when an object or painting he wanted to add to his collection came up for auction.

Northwick Gallery

I think he also appreciated that both Ernie and I were genuinely interested in the arts. I had been surrounded by good paintings all my life and had also been exposed to great paintings by Rembrandt, Vermeer, and van Gogh in the Rijksmuseum in Amsterdam, and Grecian sculptures at the Louvre. Ernie appreciated all art, but the sculptures captured his interest the most. We also learned of the captain's problems as a property owner whose income derived from the rents collected from those living on the Northwick Estate. Changing laws were altering that arrangement.

The house was unbelievably cold, and we happily crawled into our warm bed that had been heated by a hot water bottle. We were awakened at 7:00 am by a soft knock on the door, and before we could respond a young lady entered with our morning tea, seeming to ignore the occupants of the bed—a surprising but not unpleasant custom.

Breakfast was served in a miniature dining room with sterling silver food warmers on the sideboard holding a sumptuous breakfast. We learned that other guests would come for lunch before our departure, which would be served in the formal dining room. I had found pictures of the more formal rooms of the house and realized, after viewing the simple décor in the dining room, that the captain's priority was not nor ever had been to restore the house to its former splendor. He had probably converted some of the simple servants' quarters to suit his lifestyle. At lunch, the friendly guests appeared in their warmest tweed clothing, and we dined to good conversation and a simple repast and then departed, as the captain expressed the hope that we would return someday.

I have two items in my home that were gifts from Captain Churchill. He had sent a beautiful multicolored box home with

Churchill honored in book; gifts of salt shaker & box

Ernie for his mother and given us a sterling silver sugar shaker as a wedding present. They remind me of our extraordinary stay at Northwick. When the captain died in 1964 and his collection went up for sale, Ernie sent a small sum of money to the auction house to purchase an item from the estate. We waited months, and when a square-foot-sized, very light parcel finally arrived, the five of us gathered on our staircase to open our treasure. It was stuffed with paper, but we finally came upon a 3.5" Egyptian faience of the figure Horace. Our daughter Lynn just loved this piece, and we gave it to her to keep when she had her own home.

We spent another couple of weeks on this England trip visiting Stratford-on-Avon, Chipping Campden with its thatched roofs, and Wells, where we viewed a magnificent cathedral and heard the beautiful voices of a boys' choir. We also saw Windsor Castle and were impressed by the proud residents and workers of magnificent London.

Daniel, Lynn, Nancy, Ernie, 1963

Chapter Seven
Travels with Children

FROM HOME, WE TOOK one-day road trips for which I had to prepare picnics, with the chopped egg sandwiches that were my children's favorite. Invariably, within fifteen minutes of leaving the island of Montreal, my little group claimed that they were starving. But when Ernie decided to take Daniel on a camping trip, I decided to drive with my two girls to New York. From what the men told us of their adventure, we concluded that they learned to redirect the interest of bears not only from their provisions, but also helped rescue all the food of fellow campers and protected themselves as well as a group of young ladies from being eaten alive. They never went camping again.

Our road trip became exciting for Lynn and Nancy when suddenly they were able to listen to the music of the Beatles on US radio stations! They loved it! These were very strange sounds to my ears; I loved the music of the big bands we danced to and the wonderful jazz of Ella Fitzgerald, Peggy Lee, and pianists like Oscar Peterson. Nancy recalls staying at the Barbizon Plaza Hotel, shopping at Bloomingdale's, and visiting the circular Guggenheim Museum built by Frank Lloyd Wright—and that we were the lucky ones not having to fight off bears.

In 1963, Ernie and I decided that our children should experience the vastness of the land they lived in. We journeyed for three days on the Canadian Pacific Railway from Montreal to Calgary. There we attended the annual Calgary Stampede and rented a red convertible, because the children had always begged us to buy one. We drove to

Jasper National Park, where we saw one bear and one moose sitting on the side of the road as if they had been planted to make sure that tourists would not complain about the lack of wildlife roaming the park. We stayed two nights in one of Canada's grand Canadian Pacific Hotels at Lake Louise, surrounded by the massive Rockies. These enormous stone walls cannot be compared to the Alps, which are just as impressive but much gentler in appearance.

Ernie and I attempted to play golf on the resort's challenging course, but a huge thunderstorm interfered. I knew that metal cleats can attract lightning, so like a dummy, I walked barefoot back to the hotel carrying my shoes! Our fifteen-year-old Lynn created her own thunderstorm; she was in tears because she was tired of being with the family and missed her friends. We did not succumb to the moods of a young teenager but continued onward to what was supposed to be a respite from our family togetherness. Ernie had cleverly planned for us to spend three days on a range in Kamloops, British Columbia, where the children would participate in programs geared for their age groups and we would join activities available for the older folks, which included being on horseback for hours daily and resulted in sore backsides. Many of the "older folks" also saw fit to start all activities with cocktails at 10:00 am, and we sometimes joined in.

The three days passed quickly, and good humor was restored. We then drove through the fertile Okanagan Valley toward Vancouver, where the children were happy to see the red convertible returned to the rental agency. They had been exposed to more wind and sun than is comfortable and never again asked us to buy a convertible. We explored Vancouver, where I was happy to reconnect with my bridesmaid, Naomi Fitch, now an eminent physician, who toured that beautiful city with us. But upon boarding the ferry that would take us to Victoria, our last destination, a young boy appeared, someone the children had met in Kamloops. He had decided that he just must see Nancy again. Was this a sign that we were about to enter a new phase in our children's lives?

We much admired Victoria, a harbor city, with a lovely museum and the well-known Empress Hotel. But the Butchart Gardens several miles away was a highlight. In 1906, the creative Jenny Butchart decided to convert a former lime quarry into a sunken garden. After decades of a great deal of work, her dream became a reality. We were all so impressed to see how an eyesore can be converted to such magnificence. I do believe our children enjoyed this journey as I had enjoyed those on which my parents took me. As an adult, I perceived things differently. Having lived my first thirteen years in countries where if you left one town, the next was no more than five kilometers away, the distance between cities and the variety and majesty of Canada impressed me enormously.

In 1963, when we traveled this country, it had a population of less than two people per square kilometer—there was room for so many more people. Its twelve largest cities clung close to the US border. Several hundred miles to the north, the climate is too harsh for settlements; nonetheless, during the next almost sixty years, Canada's population doubled.

In addition to a taste for travel, we believed that we gave the three young Sabloffs opportunities to develop their talents, just as my parents had given me. The girls took piano lessons from such an inspiring teacher that I decided to take lessons as well. Playing that instrument was Lynn's greatest joy throughout her life. She also enjoyed learning calligraphy and would use that talent to write our twenty-fifth wedding anniversary invitations. At camp, she learned to water ski and it became her favored sport because of the feeling of flying, gliding over the water with the wind in your face.

Nancy showed herself to be multitalented. She was seven years old when, as a little Spanish dancer, she clicked her castanets on the stage of a theater filled with hundreds of people. She could sing, learned to play the classical guitar, and eventually her drawings created a portfolio that allowed her to attend Pratt Institute in New York. She learned to work with clay at summer camp and made her first ceramic vase which, although glued together after the many times it tumbled, continues to grace my porch. She still practices that craft today. All three children marched from classes in their Protestant school to the synagogue's Hebrew school. They complained a great deal about that obligation and felt that the instruction could have been better.

Daniel loved sports. Hockey was his favorite game, and he eventually learned to play the gentlemanly game of golf, at which he excelled and still plays today. Our game on my birthday became a tradition, although I believe that game we played on November 13, 2019 may have been my last. He plays an extraordinary game of Scrabble because his vocabulary is enormous. Our handsome young son studied arduously for his bar mitzvah. He read his portion

Daniel Sabloff bar mitzvah, 1967

with such poise that his family, as well the rest of the congregation, were in awe of his performance. It was, however, the end of his Jewish studies. Ernie also wisely hired a learned person to expose Daniel to different publications expressing opposing opinions, so he would learn there is always more than one side to every story.

These three were no angels, however, and caused us many sleepless nights as we lived through the '60s and '70s. There just is no end to parenting once you give birth to a child. I will share their joys and feel their pain for the rest of my days. Daniel, Nancy and I agree, however, that this is my story. Although they are still a major part of my life today, they will tell their own stories, when they desire to put pen to paper. Lynn, unfortunately, could not be part of that decision, as she tragically suffered an untimely death in 2016.

Chapter Eight
The Sixties and Seventies

THE IDEAS PROMOTED in the 1960s brought major changes in the social and political norms we had been guided by and had great consequences for my family. The *US News* reporter Kenneth Walsh wrote an op-ed in March 2010 entitled "The 1960s: A Decade of Promise and Heartbreak." He explained that it was a decade of extremes, of transformational change and bizarre contrasts: flower children and assassins, idealism and alienation, rebellion, and backlash.

We followed Dr. Martin Luther King as he led the Civil Rights Movement's massive march on Washington; President Kennedy's negotiation with the Russian leader, Khrushchev, over the Cuban Missile Crisis; the space race and events such as the love-in at Woodstock; the American folk music revival introduced by the likes of Joan Baez, Bob Dylan, and Pete Seeger; and we became aware of initial developments in the computer industry. But it was the women's liberation movement and the anti-Vietnam War demonstrations that affected my girls and made me sit up and take stock.

I only found out much later that Nancy took part in some of those demonstrations while at college in New York. We were concerned that the dormitories at Pratt were coed and wondered how liberal and trusting we could be. I had been to a lecture at Concordia University on the advent of the pill, but never took the initiative to provide them to my girls. I was not emancipated or smart enough to take that action. The Vietnam War also affected my girls in another way. How and where each of them met different groups of the more than 40,000 draft dodgers who escaped from the US to Canada I cannot recall, but those associations were not the norm for Jewish girls in Montreal.

Lynn, Daniel, Nancy

In the early '70s, when someone asked me, "And what do you do?" I realized that the question was clearly not about what occupied my time as a wife, a homemaker, a mother of three and a volunteer, but what paid work I was engaged in. My reaction was to collect all the documents of my college credits from Macdonald College and the courses that I had taken at Concordia and to register there to complete my degree, not in Agriculture but in Applied Social Science. Ernie promptly registered for two courses as well: he had always been interested in oceanography, and also decided that exposure to the computer sciences would give him insight into how the world would communicate in the future. He became a frustrated Fortran student.

One of the most beneficial courses in my discipline was "reflective listening." We were drilled in actively listening to another person and then letting that person know what we heard them say, as well as reflecting the feeling with which it was related. I feel that this kind of interaction could benefit everyone but should certainly be taught to our doctors, lawyers, and others who need a clear understanding of the problems they are asked to solve. The media course on my curriculum was my favorite. I learned to make slide presentations, a skill that would allow me to make a slideshow of my mother's life for her eightieth birthday and to present the pictures we took of our interesting journeys, using our living room wall as a screen. In 1979, I waltzed around in my cap and gown as if I had won the lottery…but now I had to find a paying job to prove that I was worthy to receive a salary. A fellow graduate and social worker suggested that we approach our synagogue, to engage them in creating a much-needed program for our seniors and others in the neighborhood.

The Leisure Institute of the Shaar Hashomayim attracted so few people upon its creation that I would have abandoned it had it not been for my mentor, Lily Katovsky, who claimed that such a program takes time to grow. It was a painstaking process, but after three years of concerted effort it grew into a going concern whose

Liesel the graduate

leadership could be taken over by another person. It is still an integral part of the synagogue today and my close, longtime friend, Naomi Kassie, now also a nonagenarian, has successfully run and expanded the program on a voluntary basis for years, with the help of donations of the synagogue membership.

Now that Ernie was well established and our children were all old enough to attend summer camp, we, like my parents, joined the all-Jewish Elm Ridge Golf Club, established in 1924. The Montreal Jewish community's interest in the game supported two other clubs as well. Elm Ridge, due to its growing membership, needed to expand its facilities and bought a piece of land on L'Île Bizard, a small island to the north of Island of Montreal, where two eighteen-hole courses were built. The Royal Montreal course, which was restricted, was also located on the island. That club has hosted the Canadian Open numerous times. Although my mother saw to it that I learned most other sports, she had not exposed me to golf, so Ernie and I took lessons and spent a great deal of time on the practice tee to develop the ability to stand in one place and swing a long stick, in exactly the right arc, to hit a small ball.

We persevered and now could join others in this game I learned to love. It is the only sport I know in which you must follow so many rules and, if you break one, announce that you have done so.

You become you own referee. In addition, golf demands that one is respectful of one's fellow players—not moving or talking when they prepare to take a swing. And all this takes place in the most beautiful surroundings while walking five or six miles, if you can, or riding a golf cart. I was hooked, especially after I hit my first hole in one! I was a rank beginner and hit a terrible shot to a par three that bounced from a water sprinkler onto a cement structure, which projected it onto the green where it found the hole. The other five holes in one I have had were more accomplished, but that first one made me believe it was possible every time I approached a par three! I was so glad that Daniel also loved this gentlemanly game, and he became so accomplished that one year he won the Junior Championship. But what I experienced watching him play his final match made me ashamed of myself and aware of how parents feel who watch their children play sports. As he was about to make a shot, I felt an anxiety I had never experienced before nor want to ever experience again, and I wished his nice, accomplished opponent only the worst.

We spent so many pleasant years socializing and playing golf with other club members, including people I had met at Camp Hiawatha as a teenager and many who were members of our synagogue and longtime friends, such as the Hirscheimers, Kassies and Issenmans. Being able to join my parents, now nine-holers, was also special. Several years after we became members, I was asked to become the vice-captain of the Ladies' Club, which had approximately 350 members but only around eighty active golfers who participated in the tournaments. I was honored and accepted. Later, I became captain and remained active in that club until we departed to live in the US in the '80s. Those experiences were to stand me in good stead when I joined the Pasatiempo Golf Club in Santa Cruz, CA.

Chapter Nine
Travels to Hydra and Israel

OVER THE COURSE of four decades, Ernie and I traveled to Israel five times and witnessed the miraculous development of this tiny nation, and I traveled once by myself in 2004. For our first trip together in 1962, we traveled with Ruth and Edgar Cohen. We decided to first explore Greece and visit Edgar's cousin, the writer, poet, and singer Leonard Cohen, who had found his Shangri-la on the small island of Hydra with Marianne at his side. The hydroplane deposited us at a restaurant where it seemed that local fishermen, having completed their work for the day, were imbibing copious amounts of alcohol. That, followed by great swarms of wasps, made us ladies want to depart immediately.

But there was Leonard, coming to greet us and beckoning us to climb the steep hill toward his home. There were no cars on the island; then and even today, donkeys and bicycles are the only mode of transportation. His home was a simple whitewashed house which he hoped to enlarge, overlooking the blue Aegean Sea. Our visit was very pleasant. It was on this island that Montreal's native son, who used to live around the corner from me, wrote two novels that were not well received by the Montreal Jewish community. Both Leonard and his contemporary, the writer Mordechai Richler, did not paint a favorable picture of Jewish life in their hometown. In reaction to the movie *The Apprenticeship of Duddy Kravitz*, based on Richler's novel, Ernie and I decided to invest in the making of a film called *Lies My Father told Me*, portraying the Jewish immigrant struggles in a more positive light. It came out in 1975 and can still be viewed on Netflix.

It was at a poetry reading of Leonard's work, later in Montreal, that I recognized his talents. I enjoyed that evening even more than listening to his songs. As Leonard matured, his popularity increased exponentially; he became a superstar not only on this continent but also around the world. When he passed away at eighty-two, he was memorialized in many countries. Today the Montreal community cannot honor him enough. His family were members of the same synagogue where we were married, and in that beautiful sanctuary the synagogue cantor and choir performed his songs at a memorial entitled "Tower of Song" in November 2017.

Shaar Hashomayin, Sabloff wedding & Cohen tribute

We departed Greece and boarded the plane to visit Israel for the first time. Flying south over its northern border toward Ben Gurion Airport near the centrally located city of Tel Aviv—one-third of the length of the country—took fifteen minutes. Israel is only 290 miles long; it is 85 miles across at its widest and only 11 miles at the narrowest part. The challenge of keeping control of this small territory, home since 1948 to a diverse population of Jews, requires constant vigilance with a well-trained and equipped defense force, which is why the Israeli Defense Force (IDF), enacted a law in 1949 that requires all eighteen-year-old males to serve for 36 months and females for 24 months. Upon our arrival at the airport and everywhere we traveled in Israel, it was, nonetheless, a surprise to see Jewish soldiers carrying guns.

Our first stop was Tel Aviv, which in 1948 had a population of 224,000 and at the time of my last visit in 2004 was a city of 804,000 people. In 2020, it was a vibrant metropolis where 4,181,479 people live. We toured this "White City" with its Bauhaus and art deco structures and visited the adjacent ancient Arab town of Jaffa. But we spent most of our time visiting with Ruth's colorful Uncle Reuven and his family who, like my cousins, had settled in Haifa, a haven where they enthusiastically participated in building this nation. The fact that we were visiting a land almost entirely inhabited by Jewish individuals was mind blowing. They had come from different countries and spoke various languages; some were Ashkenazi Jews, others followed the Sephardic tradition; many were Orthodox, and a substantial number were secular Jews. The government had to devise programs to overcome the prejudices and difficulties that often existed, such as the idea that a daughter of a Polish family would marry a young man from Iraq; or the question of how to assimilate a poverty-stricken Yemenite woman into modern society who does not speak Hebrew, has never attended a school, handled money or even taken a bus, while her young children adapt very quickly in their new homeland. With wonderful creative programs, Israel achieved many of its goals.

On a private tour of the Galilee, the northern part of Israel, with a knowledgeable guide, we passed through primitive Arab villages and observed that the developed land belonged to kibbutzim created by an idealistic group of Jews who, with the help of the Jewish National Fund (JNF), had bought land from the Arabs. The first kibbutz was built in 1909, and by 1962 there were more than two hundred. The JNF was also responsible for beginning reforestation of the land by making it possible for anyone to buy a tree as a meaningful gift to be planted in the name of the recipient. I am proud that six have been planted there in my name, one of which I planted myself in 1987.

The rest of our tour took us to Tiberias on the Sea of Galilee, Capernaum, an important Christian monument, and to the ancient city of Safed, where the Zohar, an ancient Jewish document of the Kabbala, had been written. After five days in Tel Aviv and traveling throughout the north, we then drove to Jerusalem to stay at the well-known King David Hotel, built by Egyptian Jews in 1931. During the Arab-Israel war in 1948, the land of Transjordan seized control of the West Bank and East Jerusalem, annexing the Old City and expelling the Jewish population in 1950. This prevented us from visiting not only the Old City but the Dead Sea and Masada as well. However, the terrace of our hotel permitted us a panoramic view of both the Old City and the Mount of Olives.

We spent the most memorable days of our stay in Jerusalem at Yad Vashem, the moving Holocaust memorial that contains a beautiful memorial hall where the only light comes from an eternal flame and the names of the death camps illuminated on the floor. That is where my grandmother is remembered. There are other areas where photos of thousands of victims hang in a beautiful domed building; a separate children's memorial; and a section in the surrounding gardens that remembers the Righteous Gentiles, including Captain Schroeder who piloted 937 Jews on board the *St. Louis* to safety during the period of Hitler's rule.

It is a unique experience to partake in the life of a city, as well as an entire nation, which stops on the Sabbath. Stores and restaurants close early on Friday afternoon, not to open again until the first star appears on Saturday. All public transportation comes to a halt except for taxis that charge 25 percent extra on Shabbat. The streets are quiet, as everyone attends synagogue and enjoys this day of rest with their families. Even visitors relax and enjoy this peaceful atmosphere. Yes, we bought souvenirs. One was a child's *kiddush* cup that I just passed on to little Ari Kraz, the grandchild of my good friends Yelena and Vladimir Kraz. As our traveler cheques were burning to be spent, I splurged and bought myself a unique Jensen watch that I treasure to this day and wear on all festive occasions, recalling where and when I bought it.

In 1967, all of Israel's Arab neighbors waged war on the tiny country. During the Six-Day War, the Israeli Army and Air Force miraculously defeated attacks by Egypt, Jordan and Syria, which enabled Israel to annex the Sinai, Gaza, the Golan Heights and, most importantly, the Old City of Jerusalem and the West Bank. We returned to Israel in the 1976 with Rabbi Shuchat and thirteen other members of our synagogue, on a forward-looking trip entitled "Israel in the Year 2000." The trip should have been entitled

"Developments in the Negev," because that is what we saw. We arrived in Jerusalem on a Friday afternoon and were introduced to Rabbi Pinchas Peli, a good friend of our rabbi, and a group of English-speaking Israelis with whom we celebrated the Sabbath and exchanged ideas.

Since our hotel was within walking distance from the Old City, we took the opportunity to see the Wailing Wall that first evening. Even I, whose spirituality is rarely aroused, was overcome by the large plaza on which stood the Second Temple wall, the Jerusalem stone beautifully lit to reflect its golden tone. It was magnificent! The next day we descended the steps to the plaza and observed the throng of mostly Orthodox men pray at the wall. Our husbands joined them, but we women could not pray at the wall. Orthodox tradition demanded that only men could wear the prayer shawl and read from the Torah, in a separate space from women. After Shabbat, we commenced our tour of the Negev, the desert that makes up 60 percent of the nation's southern portion. The first Prime Minister of Israel, David Ben-Gurion, stated, "It is in the Negev that the people of Israel will be tested. The great mission of populating the wilderness and bringing it to flourish will determine the fate of the state of Israel." He would have been proud of all that has been accomplished to make his dream come true, and I would have been proud to describe every detail of our trip, but I will just mention the names of the important places we visited and let you decide whether you wish to explore them any further.

Our first stop took us to a sheep range that had been purchased by Ariel Sharon, an army general who would become Prime Minister of Israel in 2001. We were all enchanted by his genuine, warm welcome and the pride he took not only in his range but also in the nearby town of Dimona, a large development town where immigrants from Morocco settled and helped to integrate those who came later from Ethiopia and Russia. As we drove toward Eilat, at the southern tip of Israel, we passed through Sde Boker, the kibbutz where Ben-Gurion is buried, and Ein Gedi, located in a dramatic rocky environment through which flow four streams, which were the most important sources of water before Israel built its desalinization plants. The drip system of watering that we and the rest of the world use today was patented in Israel in 1965. It allows a scant amount of water to be distributed in the most efficient manner.

Ariel Sharon speaks to our group

On either side of the road to our destination, we observed a great deal of new construction in process. In one area, a grove of olive trees was planted in the salty, sandy soil of the Negev. The olive oil industry would eventually become one of Israel's major agricultural products because the soil is so well suited for it. The Port of Eilat is situated like the point on a pencil on the Gulf of Aqaba, providing access to the Red Sea. Today it is a major resort city, but at the time of our trip it was a charming port town.

As we headed back north, we made a stop at a *moshav* (cooperative agricultural community) where they were experimenting with the hydroponic method of growing tomatoes in greenhouses. This type of community is different from a kibbutz in that the profit realized belongs to the owner of the property, whereas on a kibbutz all members share it. In a moshav, only the equipment and storage facilities are communal property.

Since Quebec was experiencing the Quiet Revolution during the time we were traveling and we were considering moving from Montreal, we inquired if we could become members of this moshav and take on the responsibility of looking after two greenhouses. The response was that one had to be under forty to qualify: we were much too old. Last, we visited Be'er Sheva, which was to become the largest city in the Negev, with the thriving Ben-Gurion University. Built in 1967, the university has been fulfilling David Ben-Gurion's dream of excellence in research, teaching, and scientific innovation, and is actively engaged in developing the Negev, Israel and the world.

During our first two trips we had only minimal interaction with the orthodox communities in Israel, therefore we responded positively to Evelyn and Sam Abramson's invitation to join them at the celebration of their grandchild's bar mitzvah in Israel in 1977. The thirteen-year-old was one of seven children that their son David and his spouse were raising in a like-minded community of other young Orthodox Americans who chose to make their primitive homes in a settlement just outside one of the Old City's gates. We had befriended this wonderful couple when they visited Mina, their distant relative and my father-in-law's second wife. We also had met David earlier, when he was a guitar-playing young man trying to find himself, like so many others who lost their direction in the '70s.

Ernie and I arrived in Israel several days before the celebration. We had been invited to stay with Arthur and Gisela Garmaise in Tel Aviv. Arthur and his sister, Ruth Issenman, grew up in a religious household in Montreal, while Gisela was born into an orthodox family. They and their daughters had "made *aliya*," the term to describe a Jew leaving the diaspora and moving to live in Israel. Arthur proudly took us on a tour of Tel Aviv's ultra-orthodox community of Bnei Brak with its synagogues and *yeshivas* (houses of study), each devoted to following a different rabbi's interpretation of the Torah. It was an active city founded by Hasidic Polish Jews in 1925 that now has a population of 208,748.

On the day of the bar mitzvah, we were advised to take a *sherut*, a communal taxi, which would take us to Mea Shearim, the ultra-orthodox community in Jerusalem near where the festivities would take place. The driver instructed us and another lady to sit in the back row of the taxi so that we would not be in touch with the Orthodox men who sat in the front rows. After the joyous coming-of-age ceremony, which took place among all the community members including a horde of young children, the grandparents, and us, we returned to Bnei Brak in another sherut and again occupied the back-row seats. The center row and seat next to the driver were occupied by three ultra-orthodox men. At a stop, another religious man wanted to enter the car. Neither of the two men in the center would allow him into the taxi. The driver instructed them to let him enter and allow him to sit in the middle seat. As soon as he was seated, the three other occupants assailed him with abuse. They accused him of thinking that his rabbi was superior to theirs and detailed all that was wrong with the Haredi community to which he belonged. They continued to insult this man throughout the half-hour journey to Bnei Brak. I understood their Yiddish due to my knowledge of German and was appalled by their behavior.

I wish that one of my favorite Orthodox rabbis, Rabbi David Hartman, whose lectures I had attended in Montreal and who established the Hartman Institute in Jerusalem in 1967, had been the occupant of my seat in that *sherut*. He would have intervened in their barrage of accusations and told them their behavior violated the commandments of ethical behavior and speech, and that they should have learned to obey in their studies. He would have reminded them that the *halacha*, the very "Laws of Jewish life" which guide people not only in the religious practices but also in behavior in day-to-day living, forbids gossip, slander, tale bearing, and putting one's fellow to shame.

I had to put this experience behind me to enjoy all the sights the Abramsons planned to show us. We went to Masada, a natural rock fortress thousands of feet above the nearby Dead Sea, where Herod the Great, King of Judea, built a castle complex in the last century BC and to which, according to Josephus, the Judeo-Roman historian, some 960 Jewish rebels escaped in 70 AD when Jerusalem was destroyed by the Romans. His story of their mass suicide on this fortress rather than succumbing to the Romans who surrounded it recently has been debunked by knowledgeable archeologists, as there is no archeological proof to verify that story.

We made our "escape" from Masada to take a dip in the Dead Sea, which is some 1340 feet below sea level and ten times saltier than the ocean. The exceedingly small Jordan River is the only source of sweet water that feeds the fast-shrinking Dead Sea. My Ernie, the very accomplished swimmer, took an unsuspecting and unwise running dive into the water, only to emerge needing medical care for the pain the salt water had inflicted on his eyes.

He was not the only injured Sabloff on this trip.

We had toured the Al-Aqsa Mosque, which is built on the Temple Mount and is the most important site for Arabs in Jerusalem; from there, Muhammed went to his hereafter. Afterward, a military friend of Sam's led Ernie and me to Ammunition Hill, where an important victory was won in 1967. Like good soldiers we followed our general up the hill, but at one point my ankle gave way and I sat down in pain. A cursory examination was made of my injury, and I was told to get up like a brave military recruit and march on.

I next found myself in the emergency ward of a hospital where I was bandaged and told to stay off my feet. My husband now had to push me up and down the steps of the beautiful Israel Museum in Jerusalem in a wheelchair. I limped my way onto the tarmac to return home from another enlightening trip to Israel.

Liesel & Ernie's 25th wedding anniversary, Montreal, 1972
L to R: Fred, Lotte, Arthur, Liesel, Ernie

Chapter Ten

The Quiet Revolution
and Leaving Montreal

THE QUIET REVOLUTION that began in the province of Quebec in 1960 and led to our departure for the US had repercussions that people still feel today.

The liberal Quebec government of the 1960s realized that major changes needed to be made in the Catholic educational system to allow the province's French-speaking population to learn the hard sciences and economics that the church deemed unnecessary. They raised the mandatory school age from fourteen to sixteen and created the CEGEPs, adding two more years of schooling after high school. The goal of these measures was to help the French workforce become part of an economy in which they no longer were "slaves to the English," as Premier of Quebec René Lévesque characterized the situation in 1980.

They also enacted other forward-looking programs that would become laws, such as the Quebec Pension Plan, of which I am a beneficiary even today. They joined the National Medicare Plan that went into effect in 1964, despite it being strongly contested by most physicians. In addition, they took measures to increase Quebecois control over the province's economy by nationalizing Hydro-Québec, the lucrative power company.

Unfortunately, the FLQ, or Quebec Liberation Front, a paramilitary arm of the Quebec sovereignty movement that abhorred Anglo-Saxon imperialism and wanted Quebec to separate from Canada, committed 160 violent incidents that killed eight people between 1963 and 1970. They bombed three mailboxes in 1963, one of which was a block from our house. In retrospect, it seems strange that those of us who left for greener pastures as well as warmer weather in the '80s did not pick ourselves up and go, there and then. Yet, the other incidents had no direct effect on our lives. We were also excited about the promising activities that our energetic and creative Mayor Jean Drapeau initiated and brought to fruition.

An underground subway system was completed by the time Montreal hosted the fabulous 1967 World's Fair, Expo 67. Place des Arts, with its new concert hall, was ready to receive the young Zubin Mehta, who led the Montreal Symphony Orchestra to world class status. The director of the MSO described Mehta with the following quote: "When a comet goes through your life, you do not have to be a genius to realize it." The mayor was also responsible for the renaissance of Old Montreal and recommended that the National Baseball League grant Montreal a franchise, which brought the first black baseball player, the famed Jackie Robinson, to play for the Montreal Expos.

On the national scene, Pierre Elliott Trudeau, the well-educated, worldly, and charismatic French-Canadian father of the present Prime Minister, was elected in 1968 and led Canada through the next twelve years. He proposed a twofold strategy to improve federal-provincial relations. He set forth a policy of official bilingualism, the Official Languages Act, which was passed in 1969 to make Canada a bilingual nation. A renewed Constitution with an inserted Charter of Rights and Freedoms was tabled until 1982, when it finally passed. These efforts appeased the French population and calmed the English until René Lévesque appeared on the scene as a dynamic leader. He created and led the Party Quebecois with separation from Canada as its goal. Members of the Jewish community were concerned about these unsettling activities, but there were other problems to be taken care of as well.

As part of a group of Ashkenazi Jews (as most Montreal Jews defined themselves), Ernie and I were asked to meet with several dozen of the 20,000 Sephardic French-speaking Jews who had immigrated from Morocco. The purpose of these gatherings was to familiarize these newcomers with how the Montreal Jewish community functioned, just as my parents had to familiarize themselves when they arrived in Canada. We enjoyed these encounters and were delighted to get to know these charming people and to partake in their different celebrations of the Jewish holidays. The Jewish community was also concerned that, since they were Francophones, they would more easily assimilate into the French milieu. That has not happened. Today, they make up a strong arm of the Jewish community in Montreal. Concerned Jewish citizens also played a disproportionate role in welcoming the Vietnamese "boat people." We were part of a group that sponsored a family to give these ambitious and grateful people a fresh start in life.

I joined a group of women who took it upon themselves to protest for the rights of Russian Jewry who wanted to leave their restricted lives for greater opportunity. On June 17, 1974, the Bolshoi Ballet was scheduled to perform in Montreal's concert hall. Twelve of us dressed in black bought front row seats that we occupied only until the lights were dimmed, at which time we got up and walked out,

leaving only a man dressed in prisoner's clothing standing in our seats. The audience was shaken by this small but dramatic event and the Montreal press devoted almost equal space to our demonstration as to its review of the performance.

Bolshoi Ballet protest, Montreal 1974

For me, as for so many others, the struggle for freedom for the 2,150,000 Jews who lived behind the Iron Curtain and wanted to leave Russia was a rallying point. Concerned members of our faith everywhere lobbied the American government to assist in this cause. Jews who did not dare demonstrate or protest the actions of

Nazi Germany in the 1930s were emboldened to make their voices heard about the US Jackson-Vanik amendment, which linked trade benefits for the Soviet Union to relaxing restrictions on the emigration of Soviet Jews.

A list of refuseniks—those whose applications for exit visas had been refused—was made available, which allowed concerned Jews everywhere to communicate with them. We also sent parcels with items they could use or sell to support those who were dismissed from their jobs when they applied for visas. Our now-close friends, Vladimir and Yelena Kraz, who were refuseniks, told us that the anonymous parcels they and others received were a godsend. One parcel contained a men's jacket that kept Vladimir warm in winter.

B. Issenman, Noel & Miriam Fishman

Miriam and Dr. Noel Fishman, whom we learned to love, demonstrated in San Francisco, and Miriam wrote supportive letters to refuseniks. Noel put pen to paper on University of California, San Francisco stationery to write Soviet leaders Andropov and Brezhnev, asking for freedom for Russian Jews to emigrate.

The Issenmans' daughter-in-law not only visited Ella, a distant cousin in Ukraine, but invited her to come to Canada. She hoped to be able to obtain a Canadian visa for Ella, but her interfaith marriage made that impossible. Then in 1989, when Mikhail Gorbachev and President Reagan concurred that the Berlin Wall must come down, Ella, now married to a Jewish man, was among the 1,200,000 who left Russia for Israel in the 1990s.

"Why did Russia prevent this emigration?" I was asked by my astute friend, neighbor Ken Llacera. Why indeed?

The Krazs explained: "It would be a black mark on the Soviet Union, the best country in the world, to have any person wanting to leave such a perfect environment. The Iron Curtain must not be lifted. Russians were meant to live under this illusion and never know what goes on beyond that curtain."

Yet, despite all the obstacles that had to be overcome, there were short periods of time between the '60s and the '90s during which several thousand Jews could leave the Soviet Union. By the late 1990s, 1,200,000 lived in Israel; close to 400,000 in the US; and 178,00 in Germany. In 2001, I celebrated Shabbat with a large group of Russian Jews for whom a synagogue was now under construction in my hometown, Chemnitz.

During this time, there was another important project that needed Ernie's attention. Through a client who was an international book dealer, he became aware that it was possible to acquire microfilm of ancient Hebrew documents that were of great value to scholars. The acquisition involved a complicated international procedure. Russia had made some of these microfilms available to the Vatican Library, which was now ready to sell them at a substantial cost, and Ernie became the delegated fundraiser for this project. To verify that the films were authentic, we projected samples on our dining room wall and invited noted scholars to authenticate their value. They did this with great excitement, which made us feel so proud to be part of this transaction. The money was raised, and the microfilms are now housed in the National Library in Ottawa as the Saul Hayes Collection, amongst the important Jacob Lowy Collection of ancient Jewish documents.

As the Separatist movement gained strength, my now-retired father decided to apply for visas to the US. They gave up their duplex and rented a smaller apartment, and to raise cash for this major event, sold some of their wonderful paintings to a German Jewish couple who lived in Munich but made Israel their second home. No longer Florida snowbirds but soon to become legal immigrants, they bought a condominium in Hollywood Beach, Florida where many of their friends wintered.

Both Lotte and Arthur had enjoyed good health, but as Dad approached his eighty-fifth birthday, he was troubled by a prostate problem. It could have been taken care of today, but no cure was available at that time, and he suffered periods of bleeding for several years. Leaving Canada's universal healthcare system behind forced them to pay the high insurance rates in the US; but Dad, the ultimate rational human being, explained that what he saved on taxes living in the US covered their increased medical expenses. This was another lesson for Ernie and me, who also were considering leaving Montreal.

Sadly, my Aunt Erna Becker had passed away in 1969. A few years before, I had accompanied her to the funeral of her older son Edward in Wiesbaden, Germany, the birthplace of Edward's wife, Freda von Haaren. Although Edward and Freda met in Vancouver, when Freda's psychological difficulties became apparent, they returned to Germany for medical care. After Edward's death, she inherited his estate and it was administered by her family, including Freda's brother, a Nazi officer during WW II. This was not the end of this strange turn of events. More inheritance was to come to these former Nazis twenty years later, when my brother and I were able to claim restitution for what the Beckers had lost in 1933.

Since I was the only one interested in the family treasures that traveled from Germany to Canada, I became the proud owner of Aunt Erna's unique Biedermeier-style furniture, a fabulous box of silverware for all occasions, well-worn carpets from our dining room and my father's office in Chemnitz, bronze lamps, a beautiful chandelier, and a set of Meissen dishes— all of which would eventually travel another 5,000 miles west to my European living room in California.

Biedermeier chest, sculptures by Marinsky (L) & Ernie (R) & painting from Liesel's parents

In 1977, we also sold that lovely house on Murray Hill, which held and still holds such wonderful memories of forty years of our life. The Rothschilds, Besners, Kostmans, Scherzers and Kahns were our Murray Hill family, and they and their children would always be part of my life. For the next six years we did not move too far away, renting a duplex at the bottom of Murray Park until we left for the US in 1983.

The fact that Canada was now a bilingual nation was not enough for the leaders of the Party Quebecois. By August of 1979, they had crafted Bill 101—the Charter of the French Language Act—which made French the language of business in Quebec and restricted the use of English on all signs. The game was up; we now had a language police force. Although this law had no direct effect on us, the mood that it created in the province was very unpleasant. If one inadvertently approached a Francophone for help in English at a market and received a blank stare in return, there was a feeling of unnecessary animosity. Any banks, insurance companies and other large businesses with more than fifty employees that objected to requirements to conduct all their business in French moved their assets out of the province and made plans to establish offices in Toronto, in anticipation of a downturn in Quebec's economy. Familiar street names as well as all storefronts were francized, and traffic signs would no longer give English-speaking tourists any guidance.

A 1980 referendum to determine whether the population of Quebec would agree to separation negotiations with the Canadian government was defeated. Another attempt was made in 1992 and this one was also rejected, but by a smaller number of votes. All these maneuvers prompted 224,000 English speakers to leave the province. The unemployment rate rose from 8.7 percent to 10.4 percent in 1977 and remained above 11 percent for nineteen of the last twenty-three years of the twentieth century.

We also decided to move some of our assets out of Quebec, but rather than moving them to Toronto, we transferred them to an American bank to take advantage of the exchange rate in our favor. The decision to leave Montreal was also easier for us because two of our children had settled elsewhere. Nancy was pursuing a singing and songwriter career in California. Daniel, having completed his

BA in philosophy at the University of British Columbia, settled in Vancouver. Only Lynn, who was bilingual like all our three children, stayed in Quebec. She loved Saint-Sauvere, a growing winter and summer resort in the Laurentian mountains, where she now owned a kitchenware store.

We had hoped that our offspring would find suitable mates and make us grandparents, but that sadly was not an experience that would be granted to us, and we finally came to terms with it. As I was writing the above, I received my daily call from my now sixty-six-year-old son and questioned him, as I have questioned myself so often: "What could your dad or I have done differently?" He responded, "Nothing, Mom, we were influenced by the times in which we grew up."

Ernie's brothers and their families now also lived in the US, each having married American citizens, and I know of only one Sabloff grandchild born to my niece, Ina. My brother remained single all his life, and since my two cousins had passed away leaving no progeny, I had to accept the fact that the Becker genes were not going to be reproduced—unlike so many other Holocaust survivors who thankfully bore children to carry on the Jewish tradition.

Having made the decision to leave Quebec, we then had to decide where to make our new home. We knew that spending the winters in Florida or making it our permanent residence was not an option. To us, it was a hot and humid place where people moved to watch their lives wind down, and we still wanted and felt capable of becoming an integral part of a community. Our friends Ruth and Bernie Issenman introduced us to a community where this might be possible.

Our plans were linked to this devoted couple with whom we had studied the Bible for many years, traveled to numerous countries, and enjoyed three stints at different Club Meds. We often joked about the frightening adventures we shared, such as being completely fogged in on the ski slopes of St. Moritz, or when we attempted to navigate the ice-covered roads near their house in Vermont, or driving Highway 52 in California during an immense lightning storm. Bernie was both mentally and physically as strong as the Rock of Gibraltar. He adored his wife, Ruth, a Judy Garland look-alike. She was lively and loved interesting conversations and discussions, and was a completely devoted mother to their four children: Phillip, Bob, Candy, and Tina.

The Issenmans decided that if they moved from Quebec, it would be to Santa Cruz, California where their daughter Candy had settled with her husband, Neal Coonerty, to run Bookshop Santa Cruz, today one of the most treasured landmarks of that city. In preparation for this move, they bought the historic Mackenzie House in the golfing community of Pasatiempo in the latter part of the '70s. Alister Mackenzie was the highly regarded architect of this community's golf course and, more importantly, the architect of the Augusta National where the Masters tournament is played, as well as other well-known courses throughout the world. The Issenmans loved history and treasured the house, not only for its location and comforts but also for the story it tells.

When they extended their hospitality to us, we readily accepted. As our hosts drove us down the magnificent coastal highway from San Francisco to laid-back Santa Cruz, with its unique University of California built on a hilltop in the redwoods, we could not get over the beauty of the area. Although Pasatiempo seemed like an ideal community for us, we decided that if California was to become our new home, it would be wise to take a trip from San Diego and explore other coastal communities to assure ourselves that there was nothing as attractive to us. We were easily convinced that not only was Pasatiempo the most attractive, but also learned from one of the Issenmans' neighbors who had committed himself to an extensive study of climates that this was one of the best in the world. He did not warn us that we would also live close to one of the earth's largest and most dangerous faults.

Even if we had been aware of that, we would not have been deterred. The die was cast. To establish a foothold in the US, we bought a small house on Baltusrol Drive in nearby Rio del Mar that we rented out. When we were finally ready to move, we sold that house and bought one in Pasatiempo. Since we were not the kind of homeowners who were interested in changing the configuration of a house, opening walls, or installing an entirely new kitchen, we eventually sold that house, and in 1982, our happy, patient realtor found 49 South Circle, which suited us perfectly and required no alterations. Ernie agreed with my decisions but could have been comfortable anywhere, because he believed that our move to Santa Cruz was a move to paradise.

We filed our visa applications, but it would take at least five years before the US would admit both the Issenmans and us, though we would not deprive anyone of a job and would happily pay our annual taxes. While we waited, Ernie, who was bilingual, had no difficulties continuing his practice; I was able to see the Leisure Institute become an integral part of the synagogue. It was a satisfying experience to know that I had been part of creating something that bore fruit. And, of course, I had a response to the question "And what do you do?" of which I was proud.

We made plans to celebrate my mother's eightieth birthday on January 31, 1981. My slideshow of her accomplishments—as a member of the community, the sports she pursued, as a valued friend and beloved wife and mother—was ready for presentation. But unfortunately, all those plans had to be cancelled a week before the party when my dear dad was taken to the hospital with prostrate problems that had become unmanageable. When we arrived to visit him and told him of our plans, hoping to divert him from his problem, he calmly explained that he could not focus on our plans and wished us well in all we were doing. My very caring, now altered father had tuned out. He knew a cure was not possible and he was moving on, in a way that he and my mother had anticipated and discussed.

The day he was released from the hospital, we gathered for dinner in my parents' apartment. I was still hoping to cheer my father up and suggested that we watch the slideshow, but he remained unmoved and wanted to retire. To this day I do not know if he discussed his plans for that night with my mother, but when I went in to say good night, I knew that he was readying himself to take enough pills to end his life. He did not want to subject himself or my mother to the constant physical and medical attention he would inevitably need.

I suggested that he give it some more thought and he responded, "If you take the bottle of pills away, I will jump out the window." I then said good night as well as goodbye, not only to my wonderful father but to one of the kindest, capable, most principled men I have known throughout my entire life. My mother was remarkably calm during these trying days, but after weeks the reality of her loss caused this otherwise extremely social lady to have worrisome periods of depression. The right doses of medication helped her overcome this time of grief, and after approximately six months, she was able to resume all her activities with her usual spirit and interest.

Lotte also had a great knack of finding the right help she needed during the next twenty years of her life, which made life for my brother and myself so much easier. My father had confidence in my ability to make sure that my mother's finances would be well looked after. His estate was so uncomplicated that my task, with the help of his lawyer and accountant, was not burdensome. Yet the responsibility to ensure that her assets were safely allocated with the best rate of return kept me on my toes. Both Aunt Hertha (my mother's widowed sister-in-law) and my mother-in-law now also turned to me for financial advice. I should have studied financial management instead of farming or applied social science.

Above, Pasatiempo California home; below, horse sculpture by Ernie

Chapter Eleven
Adieu Montreal; Hello California!

THERE WAS MUCH to take care of before we moved to California, and Ernie found that the stress took a toll on his memory. He decided to take a course to address the problem. Unfortunately (and most unlikely), the instructor forgot to attend the first session, and that was the end of that endeavor.

Ernie's top priorities were to make sure that his former clients were well served after his departure, and to deliver his life's work to the storage facility of the Notarial Board. Basil Ballon, our competent friend and a fellow notary who shared Ernie's office space, agreed to look after his clients and, under my husband's careful supervision, he and I boxed 26,000 deeds in numeric order so that others could easily access the information.

Since we were moving to a much smaller, 1900-square-foot house, we had to divest ourselves of our antique dining room set—a beautiful round walnut table that opened to seat twelve comfortably—that had been in our family since we first settled in Montreal in 1939. We had consumed so many thousands of meals around that friendly table, had so many important conversations, and it held so many memories, it was painful to contemplate letting it go. But to my surprise, when an Orthodox Jewish family of eight marched up our stairs to inspect my treasure and could not wait to make it theirs, I was no longer dismayed to sell it. It had found a loving home and would be the setting for more interesting and enlightening conversations and celebrations.

Now that our departure was imminent, we had to say goodbye to friends and acquaintances. Two couples—Rita and Ernie Hirscheimer and my favorite golf partner, Myrna Abbey, and her husband Stanley—each decided to have a farewell party at their homes. The albums full of pictures and good wishes of those events are on our bookshelves, and the beautiful silver *mezuzah* we were given at the Abbeys' is on the doorpost of our California living room.

Ernie's sculptures

We had ordered the moving van and packed all my German treasures as well as the handcrafted pine furniture we had hunted down on trips to rural Quebec; ten sculptures that Ernie had created; books and more books; and the liquor that had not been consumed, with an eye toward a large cocktail party in California. Still, the van was not filled to the rafters.

Throughout our thirty-three years of marriage, we had begun to appreciate the art of diverse cultures. On a trip to Mexico, Ernie bought an eight-inch pre-Columbian clay figure that seemed an unlikely addition to our collection, but we learned to love that little man just as we did the statuesque ivory Chinese figure, the African masks, Eskimo sculptures, and the lively paintings by Canadian Indian artists. My husband also enjoyed going to auctions. Some of his purchases were beautiful, but on occasion he would come home

Pre-Columbian figure

with an item that was not to my liking. So I decided to join him on these outings. At one auction, I raised my arm too high to pull back a strand of hair and inadvertently acquired a lovely little antique side table that was also going to California.

While the moving van was on its way to California, Ernie and I left on another well-planned, three-week trip across the US to see more of the country that would now be our home. Sightseeing in Chicago was one of the highlights of our journey, and we were surprised by the wonderful collection of art in its museum. Since we had never heard of Tulsa, Oklahoma before this trip, it was a revelation to drive into a beautiful environment with exquisite homes the size of small palaces, all financed by the oil found in that area over decades. Santa Fe, New Mexico, was all that Southwestern art lovers could hope to experience and more.

(While writing this, I picked up the phone to call Paul Cahn, at ninety-five the youngest of the three Cahn boys the Birks family brought to Canada so long ago. Paul has a house in Santa Fe, where I had been invited to a special birthday eight years ago. I learned that Santa Fe became an important center for the arts when scientists such as George Cowan, working in Los Alamos to create the atom bomb, founded the Santa Fe Opera and the Santa Fe Institute. Paul became an avid collector of Native American weavings, many of which he and his wife Elissa donated to the museum in St. Louis, Missouri, where they reside.)

As Ernie and I headed further west, we found ourselves driving through miles and miles of desert without a gas station in sight. I was so excited when I saw a sign suggesting that one could drive up to a mesa where Hopi Indians lived, but my usually curious husband only focused on the arrow indicating that we were running out of gas. We crossed the desert without a mishap, but I have yet to climb a mesa. After entering California through Bakersfield, with a full tank of gas, we again followed Ernie's plan. No more highways for my explorer. Via Coalinga, we drove through beautiful golden California hills where cattle lazily grazed in the shadows of the scrub oak, and finally emerged to see the Pacific Ocean.

The van arrived at our new home, and what we brought with us helped to create a comfortable atmosphere for our new nest. We furnished the guest room on the lower floor with the Canadian pine furniture for visits from our children, family members and friends. We nailed the beautiful mezuzah our friends had given us to our living room doorpost. It contains a tiny scroll of Biblical prayers inscribed with a Hebrew commandment from the Torah: "One performs a mitzvah when one writes of G-d on the gates and doorpost of your home."

I had thought that adapting to my new surroundings would be a walk in the park for someone who had done this three times before. But to my surprise, I struggled to be entirely at ease for the first few years while Ernie, so in love with his surroundings, had none of these problems. In Montreal, people had known me with all my foibles and attributes. Now I had to explain myself repeatedly to those who I met. Yet, I had looked forward to the change—from living in a completely Jewish environment to what the late William Safire, a columnist for *The New York Times*, described as "a salad bowl." He claimed, "What calls for semiotic celebration is not so much our unity as the strength and glory in our diversity."

That diversity also existed within the Jewish community of Santa Cruz. Intermarriage between couples of different religions had become a norm in the US, and in 1982, the little Temple Beth El serving the needs of sixty-seven families welcomed a sizable percentage of mixed-marriage couples. Candy, the Issenman's daughter, along with her Catholic husband, Neal Coonerty, were met with open arms, as were the Issenmans, Ernie and I. The more conservative, older members reached out to make us feel part of the community and, as time passed, we became part of a *chavurah*, a group of friends with whom we celebrated birthdays, attended symphony rehearsals in San Francisco, and confronted the challenges of life. Our little congregation grew and is now housed in a modern structure with the

Neal & Candy Coonerty

facilities needed to accommodate all who want to celebrate Jewish life.

I also realized my high hope that membership in the beautiful, challenging Pasatiempo Golf Club would become a major part of my life in Santa Cruz, but not before overcoming my doubts about whether I was welcome. There was no welcoming committee to greet newcomers to the club, and I knew from experience that golfers often form cliques with favorite partners who have similar skills. No one invited me to play, and I wondered what the reason could be for what I considered a rejection. I had long since learned, from training for my degree in Applied Social Science, that I am not the easiest person to get to know, and I decided that it was up to me to make a greater effort to be sociable. I did this, and was helped to a great degree by an article in the *Santa Cruz Sentinel* in 1985 about a meeting of the local Hadassah. The organization had invited

Whims of war and prejudice brought them to Santa Cruz

Santa Cruz Sentinel article, 1/25/85

three Jewish immigrants to talk about their heritage, and the article devoted an entire page to pictures and our stories: mine, my dear friend and Russian refusenik Yelena Kraz, and Rosa Gelfman, who had spent the war years in Shanghai, a haven from the Holocaust. I was no longer a stranger in my surroundings.

But another factor also contributed to my doubts about the degree to which we were accepted at the club. Having been a member of an entirely Jewish club in Montreal because the others were restricted, it was disturbing to learn that Pasatiempo also had been restricted at its founding in 1929. Alarm bells went off when I heard the word "restricted," and as far as I knew, I was the only Jewish woman golfer. I did not and still do not want to be anywhere near a club, hotel, or neighborhood where I am not wanted. Yet if my concerns were warranted, we would have been questioned about our religious affiliation when we bought our property and the golf club membership. That had not happened.

Nonetheless, my suspicions were not entirely unreasonable.

Despite the Civil Rights Act of 1964 prohibiting discrimination in public accommodations and federally funded programs, it was evident then and even today that the law is not strictly followed. Clubs could remain private unless they benefited from public funds. The Baltimore Country Club, which in 1970 had still not removed a sign "No Dogs, No Coloreds, No Jews," made money by hosting tournaments, and the venerable Augusta National Golf Club broke this law by hosting profitable outside tournaments such as The Masters while limiting its membership to three hundred carefully chosen male members. Not much has changed in the makeup of that membership, but as recently as 2012, Condoleezza Rice, the African American former US Secretary of State, was one of two women admitted to the club. She has now been joined by two other females and three Black men.

Yet, it was the article in the *Santa Cruz Sentinel* that opened the door for me. My life and my religious affiliation were now an open book. One year when I was not signed up for the club championship, our ladies' golf champion, Sandy Woodruff, asked me why I was not on the list. When I told I told her that the tournament fell on the holiest Jewish holiday, Yom Kippur, she immediately responded, "We will have to take that into consideration when we plan next year's tournaments."

For more than thirty-two years, I experienced immense joy playing the game I love twice weekly with wonderful people, as an active member of the Ladies Club. Those years culminated in a festive, nine-hole golf tournament on my ninetieth birthday. More on that amazing birthday later.

While I had struggled to fit into the golfing community, Ernie had no great ambition to find golfing partners other than Bernie and Joel Alexander. Joel and his wife Faye were members of our chavurah. Their casual nine-hole game satisfied Ernie completely. My husband also was enchanted by the local University of California Arboretum that is filled with species imported from other parts of the world with similar climates and soil conditions. For as long as he was able, he volunteered his time at the Arboretum, becoming protea pruner-in-chief in those beautiful hillside surroundings. When his blue eyes were not on his job, he had the pleasure of viewing the wonderful vista of the entire Monterey Bay.

Ernie always loved jazz and often visited the then-active Cooper House in downtown Santa Cruz, where musicians gathered to perform. He also was a sculptor, and had bought a large piece of marble with the intention of sculpting an African American man's head. A maquette was made, but his artistic muse seemed to have left him; he did not pick up his sculpting tools again. It was one of the early signs of the Alzheimer's disease that he would eventually have to live with.

He did, however, become my willing assistant in my ridiculously small, almost unprofitable, but very enjoyable business venture. It turned out that we had no place in our new home for the items that had traveled with us from Montreal. Since we were enamored with auctions and hunting for "antiques" (which were mostly attractive rejects), we decided I should rent a space in one of the cooperatives where different dealers set up their wares. I filled the windowless six-by-eight-foot space with our "rejects" along with other items Ernie and I found at the weekend flea market and garage sales. Traveling to remote areas to see garage sale offerings really helped us become familiar with our surroundings.

Ernie's main job in this venture was to find a specific kind of Depression glass that I love, have collected, and used a great deal throughout the years. He was also in charge of buying the tools a household needs, which this repairer uses frequently today. As we wandered through the market, two large decorative pieces of ironware that we felt would enhance the Issenmans' home caught our eyes. They agreed, and immediately hung them in prominent places.

I became an amateur restorer of frames and chairs, and even learned how to laboriously remove stains from precious china. I loved the challenge. The replacement for our dining table was hard to find, but through my connections in the Santa Cruz antique community we found an old round oak table that the creative owner transformed into an oval with three leaves, extending it to seat ten people comfortably. But that reconstruction was not all this genius accomplished. He painted it a Cadillac car paint of my choice, turning the oak a dark, lacquered maroon that fulfilled all my desires.

That table has been admired over the past thirty-eight years and has allowed me to entertain my guests with considerable pride in its beauty. If it could talk, it would tell you of the Friday night dinners I served while friends discussed the state of our world, news of their  families, or important issues in our community. Most important, however, is the night of Yom Kippur, when we gather to break the fast of that most holy day, and when we hope to be forgiven for all our sins of the previous year. Approximately twenty friends contributed to this annual feast, and Ernie and I loved to see them all interact in our new surroundings. We had achieved our aim to become part of a new community. No longer were we known as Mr. and Mrs. Sabloff; to the banker, the lawyer, the realtor, neighbors, and new acquaintances, we were Ernie and Liesel. The friendliness and informality were a delight.

In the early '80s, we celebrated the Sabbath every week at the Issenmans' home. Every Friday night, my friend Ruth showed us how to give that event special meaning, choosing a small portion of the Bible to read and explaining its relevance to each week. Her guests included her daughters Tina and Candy, Candy's husband Neal, their small children Ryan and Casey, and us. On one occasion, Ruth asked five-year-old Ryan to explain the meaning of her remarks, and without hesitation this bright little boy responded correctly. The evening also included Bernie reading the "Woman of Valor" prayer, which praises the mother of the household, and a blessing of the children read by their father. At the time, *challah*, the twisted egg bread eaten on the Sabbath, was hard to find in Santa Cruz, so I baked it. I enjoyed kneading, twisting, and baking it so we had it to bless on those evenings.

One Friday night in 1982, when Ruth and Bernie were out of town, Candy hosted the dinner. Like her parents, she invited new-comers Yelena and Vladimir Kraz, their seven-year-old Konstantin, and Yelena's mother Nina, recent immigrants and former refuseniks. From that time until today, our friendship with the Kraz family has grown into a remarkably close relationship. I have always related more easily to those who share the refugee experience. I also hoped

Yelena, Mark, Konstantin, & Vladimir Kraz celebrating citizenship

that my tiny part in demonstrating for the freedom of Russian refuseniks had made it a bit easier for this bright, young successful couple to escape the Russian menace and become a great asset to our community. Their little son Mark was born an American two years after their arrival, and it was the Krazs' fervent hope that they would reunite with the rest of their family soon.

Although Santa Cruz seemed to be off the beaten track for well-known Jewish lecturers, we had our share, and any one of us were happy to open our homes to them on Shabbat and to invite others who might be interested in the topics they wished to discuss. One evening in the '80s, the now thirty-year veteran talk show host, Wolf Blitzer of CNN, was the Issenmans' dinner guest. At that time, he was in Santa Cruz to speak to members of our temple as the Washington correspondent for the *Jerusalem Post*, the only Israeli English-language newspaper. Ernie and I hosted two other interesting speakers, one of whom would inspire us to take part in a vastly different kind of journey in 1987 as volunteers for Israel. The other came to our city to promote a movie made from a book published in 1982, based on a story told to Australian writer

Thomas Keneally (while buying luggage in a Los Angeles store) of the Holocaust survivor Leopold Poldek. For the life of me, I cannot remember if it was the luggage owner himself who was at my home or whoever was promoting the movie, but Poldek was determined to see it made. It became Stephen Spielberg's *Schindler's List*. This film should be shown annually for a week in every city of the world to remind people what can happen when a vindictive dictator assumes power, and to recognize that there are many righteous people who stand up for those that suffer.

Reconnecting with our good friends remained important throughout our entire lives together, and fortunately, we were able to welcome them in our new home. But of course, the most important visitors we welcomed with open arms were our children. When all three were able to visit at the same time, it was such fun to see them interact just like when they were young—lovingly baiting and teasing each other. Lynn did not visit often because she became ill when traveling by plane, so we spent more of our time with her

on our trips to Montreal every second year. Daniel, the golfer, loved coming to Santa Cruz. We played our twenty-five-cents-a-hole matches on the challenging Pasatiempo course and made tee times at other beautiful courses in our area. He always came in November to play with me on my birthday, and was proud to announce to the other twosomes who joined us that his mother, who had just hit a 165-yard drive, was in her eighties. This was routine until we played our final game in 2017.

Liesel & Daniel, last game

Our Nancy, at that time a singer-songwriter, knew Santa Cruz well. She had lived here for a while before we moved and had performed at the local clubs. She and her friend Ruby were depicted as "Local Ladies in Rock" on the cover of the local weekly, the *Good Times*. This success prompted her to move toLos Angeles with the hope of achieving greater success. With only one song published, she became a legal temporary worker to earn her keep, before moving to the Big Island in Hawaii to work full time with clay.

We also encouraged my mother and Aunt Hertha to visit Santa Cruz, hoping that they, too, would move here from Florida. They were here in the middle of October dressed in their warmest clothes but nonetheless were cold throughout their entire visit. I have memories of my

Lynn, Nancy, Daniel, 1980s

active mother sweeping the steady supply of oak leaves that fell on our driveway, wearing a heavy camelhair coat over her wool pants and sweater with a wool scarf wrapped around her head and neck. Though she did enjoy seeing all her old belongings being used and was happy that we had found such a good place to retire to, she and Aunt Hertha decided they were going to live out their lives among their friends in the warmth of Florida.

Our little family relied heavily on good airline connections to visit each other, and we also often continued to fly to explore far-off places.

Russia holds the title for the most beautiful metro stations in the world

Chapter Twelve
New Travel Horizons

NO ONE COULD HAVE convinced us that we could have found a better place to retire; but as much as I loved my surroundings, I also realized that we were a living in a unique little corner of the world. Whenever we returned from our travels, landing in San Jose then crossing the Santa Cruz mountains to reach our home city, I returned to my comfortable, racially homogeneous bubble, which lacks the diversity and the divides that have become so pronounced in the rest of the US and the world in general.

Leaving this bubble was one of the reasons I was excited to receive a call in 1985 from Myrna Abbey, who suggested I join her on a two-week journey to Britain and Russia entitled "The Bolshoi and The Bard." Ernie had made it clear that he did not want visit Russia or spend even one dollar of his money in that country. How did he react to my wanting to join Myrna on that voyage? He reacted as he did throughout our entire marriage; he wished me bon voyage and hoped he would not have to come and rescue me from the Russian authorities.

When I informed the Krazs that I would visit their homeland, they were excited for me and happy for the opportunity to send much-desired electronic equipment to their family. Thus, I became a smuggler of illegal goods. They were hidden in my suitcase with instructions to use a pay phone to contact the recipients—not to call them from the hotel to meet with me, in case someone might be listening. Myrna also carried gifts to a dissident couple, but her instructions were less onerous. She had been instructed to take the subway to their location, visit with them and present them their gifts—and to have the number of the Canadian embassy readily at hand in case of trouble.

Airports are wonderful places to observe the traveling public, and since I was departing from San Francisco, I noted that most of the travelers were of Asian descent. Upon my return home through London's Heathrow Airport, I saw a vast number of Pakistanis, Arabs and Black people intermingling in a multicultural atmosphere.

Myrna and I met in London, and I have racked my brain to tell you of our experiences during our stay in the Bard's country. Although I can recall precisely where I saw the great Paul Robeson in his performance of *Othello* in Montreal in the late 1940s, and when the unbelievably talented pianist Vladimir Horowitz performed in a concert there, only two memorable experiences of our time in London stand out. As there was no organized sightseeing, Myrna, proudly wearing her bright red coat, became my guide. I happily followed her to a unique art exhibit that highlighted the link of paintings by Picasso, Renoir, Degas and other well-known Impressionists with their sculpted works. While it was unusual for me to spend time at the movies while traveling, we saw *My Beautiful Launderette*, a film that broke major ground in its bold exploration of race and sexuality in multicultural London during the Thatcher era of the 1980s. The film was Daniel Day Lewis's first and I became a fan, following him throughout his career, which to date includes 212 film award nominations and 139 awards.

While Myrna spent time with a dear friend, I was happy to be able to reconnect with my mother's friend Lotte Bauman's daughter, Liesel Gotch and family, who had visited us in Bloemendaal. That short reunion evoked good memories of my life in Holland and of visits with Dutch friends over the years who also shared my childhood. Years later, Liesel and I shared the sad experience of our husbands gradually losing their memories. After their passing, we visited each other frequently until she, too, passed away in 2010.

The second week, we took a dilapidated Aeroflot plane to Russia, landing safely in Moscow. We passed successfully through customs with our contraband, but life from that moment on was under the control of an unsmiling female Intourist agent. She registered us at the primitive (by Western standards) Hotel Intourist, where the rooms were most likely bugged, and a guard-like person sat at a desk on the hallway of our floor. Yet, the hotel was well located overlooking Red Square, affording us a splendid view of Moscow's main attractions: the Bolshoi Theatre, the beautiful, brightly decorated towers of the Saint Basil's Cathedral, the Kremlin Wall, the huge GUM department store, and the well-preserved body of Vladimir Lenin, on view in his mausoleum.

We awoke the first morning to the unlikely sight of a troupe of sixteen women chatting, brooms in hand, while sweeping the square of the previous day's dirt. Machines were available, but "Everybody must be employed" was the communist motto. During the next day and a half, we toured the city, visited museums and the unbelievably beautifully decorated metro stations, and observed the lack of cultural diversity. Compared to us—well-fed Westerners used to goods and services from around the globe and information shared without hesitation—Moscow was populated with dour people afraid to converse for fear of being spied on, dressed in clean but drab clothes, on lines at bakeries, butchers, and vegetable markets in the hope of being on time to buy fresh food for their next meager meal.

Since settling into our hotel, we had searched for the coins needed to phone the Krazs' friends and relatives, but no one was willing to give me the proper change—not at the hotel nor in a bookstore we entered for that purpose. We excused ourselves from the second-day tour and decided that we would deliver the presents to the refuseniks who lived in Moscow. This meant we had to negotiate the metro, where names of the stations were all written in Russian Cyrillic script. Even after purchasing a subway guide at an outdoor magazine stand and asking them to point to the station where we should exit, they refused to give me change. *Nyet* was the answer to requests for coins.

I made a final attempt by asking, "Sprechen sie Deutsch?" With this, the saleslady's demeanor changed radically. I continued that I was from eastern Germany, at which point she smilingly gave me the much-needed coins. Yet, those precious coins just caused me more frustration. The people I called in Moscow could not see a safe way to meet with me. When I finally reached Yelena's sister in Leningrad, she, too, was noncommittal and said she would try to connect with me when we visited the Hermitage Museum.

But Myrna was able to call to confirm that the recipients of her gifts were ready to see us. The husband greeted us at the exit of the subway station and walked us to one of five-story *Krushchyovka*—cement-slab apartment buildings built during the Khrushchev era to house those who left the land to work in the city. Yelena had recently told me that she, her mother, and her sister each lived in one of those and that *Krushchyovka*, a combination of Khrushchev and slum, did not describe them correctly. According to her, they were a significant improvement over the communal living arrangement in older apartments. These same drab *Khrushchyovka* were built throughout the entire Communist bloc, and I would see them in my hometown of Chemnitz in the '90s.

His wife welcomed us to their crowded one-room apartment where, over tea, they shared their frustrations with trying to emigrate, being refused, and losing their jobs in retaliation. They expressed their deep gratitude for all the support and gifts they had received from the West and their continued hope of being able to leave Russia soon. Satisfied to have accomplished even one mission, we rejoined our group for dinner. I ate more borscht, mashed potatoes, and cucumber during this Russian tour than I have in the years thereafter. The anticipated performance of ballet at the Bolshoi was a disappointment. Our seats, toward the back of this enormous theater, allowed us only to see the dancers clearly with an opera glass, and even so, it in no way compared to the performance I had seen in Montreal with one of their finest performers, Maya Plisetskaya.

We were happy to leave Moscow for Leningrad, which I believe to be one of the beautiful cities of the world. It came as a pleasant surprise that our accommodations in the up-to-date Park Inn, a 1500-room hotel built by Swedes in the '70s, were extremely luxurious. The hotel, however, was as far as possible from the center of the city to prevent tourists from mingling with the locals. I threw caution to the wind and called Yelena's sister, Inna, from the hotel phone to determine if she still planned to meet me at the Hermitage and received a noncommittal reply: She might be able to meet me at the coat check counter during the next two days, around 2:00 pm. That did not happen, although for two days I was a suspicious person with a knapsack filled with gifts on my back. I was uncomfortable checking it in at the wardrobe, where it was received with questioning eyes, and when I retrieved it after our second visit to the museum, I became aware that I was being followed.

My gait is generally slow, but I now walked very briskly to escape and boarded the bus that would take me back to the safety of the hotel. I had the rest of that afternoon and evening to reflect on what we had seen in this "Venice of the North" on the river Neva, with its interesting architectural structures, some of which mixed Russian with French characteristics. The French influence was pronounced in the Russian Royal Courts. At the time of our visit, the beautiful cathedrals, churches, and synagogues were devoid of parishioners. Religion and communism did not mix. It seemed incongruous, however, to see people working with small paintbrushes and gold leaf to restore the splendor of the churches, Catherine the Great's palace, and the frames of the windows of the Hermitage Museum. I should not have been surprised that they took considerable pride in these edifices, since most of the countries I have visited treasure the splendor of their past despite despising those who may have created them.

The magnificent Hermitage, a former palace, housed an enormous collection of great paintings and sculpture but needed a competent curator. One cannot appreciate a great Rembrandt painting hung in a confined, unlit corner. Myrna and I were both blown away, however, by a simple room on the third floor that housed approximately twenty of the most magnificent Impressionist paintings. Although our guided tour allowed only ten minutes with them, we returned to the museum the next day to view them at our leisure. It made us wonder how these more modern paintings got to Russia. Today we know that not only these twenty but also fifty others in the museum's storeroom were stolen from German collectors during WW II. The Russians had and still have no intention of returning them to the families of their rightful owners.

At dusk that evening, I received a message that someone was coming to meet me in the large plaza in the front of the hotel and there was Inna, somewhat nervous. I had gone through unnecessary traumas to make the delivery of these gifts, yet I was delighted to report to my friends that they were now in the right hands.

On the day of our departure, Myrna decided we had to shop at the local GUM department store to buy souvenirs. While she went to use the facilities, she asked me to hold her red coat, which had attracted covetous glances throughout our trip. Suddenly I was surrounded by people who wanted to buy that coat. Fortunately, Myrna returned before it was torn from my arms.

Myrna Abbey, Russia

As we boarded the plane, we felt relieved that we were no longer seen as spies or felt our reluctant hosts spying on us. Myrna was able to be her affable, expressive self again and we shared our sadness at how the Russian people were kept from living the rich life that we live in the West. The Krazs could tell you the amazing sense of freedom that emigration to the West has given them and how it allows them—a creative electronic engineer and his bright wife—to contribute to the US economy, although adapting to life in this country meant relearning things, among them how to shop. On one of his first attempts to buy vinegar at Safeway, Vladimir stood in front of that selection of vinegars not knowing which to choose among six or more assorted types. Which one would Yelena like? In Russia, one could only hope that even one kind would be available. Today their American cupboard holds as many kinds of vinegar as I have in mine.

Until my mother, the volunteer extraordinaire, visited in Santa Cruz, I had not tried to volunteer for any service that would give back to the community that took us in. I decided to train to become a docent at the local art museum, which at that time occupied the second floor of the Santa Cruz Library. I benefited more from this experience than the community did, by exposure to American artists of that era such as Wayne Thibaud of California, Georgia O'Keeffe of New Mexico, and the creations of Judy Chicago. Having acquired skills in assisting others to improve their interpersonal relationships, I also joined a group trained in conflict resolution, to help people resolve their differences before disputes escalated into legal issues.

At one point, I created a volunteer position for myself in the emergency department of Dominican Hospital. Having experienced the inefficiency of the intake staff, I felt that a volunteer could help determine which patients were at risk of serious trauma and needed immediate care and which could wait. None of my efforts were long lasting because, in the latter half of the '90s, a job was created for me: I became my husband's caregiver. But we still had a few years before that happened, and the most enjoyable volunteer experience lay ahead of us.

In November of 1987, we celebrated Ernie's seventieth birthday with our children in Big Sur, a beautiful spot on the California coast. About the same time, an emissary of Israeli General Aharon Davidi, who headed the Volunteers for Israel program, spoke to a group at our home, hoping to enlist lovers of that state in a three-week work program in the Israeli Army. The program began in 1982, during the first war with Lebanon, when Israeli farmers in the Golan Heights faced the prospect of losing their crops, as most able-bodied men and women had been called into the army and the ripening crops were left unattended. Six hundred volunteers from the US were recruited to come to Israel, and the crops were saved. These people found the experience so rewarding that they formed groups in regions across the US. Since then, thousands of volunteers have signed on to work on Israel Defense Force (IDF) bases.

Ernie was hooked, but when he revealed his age, he was told he was too old. My law-abiding husband fought that restriction, and with the General's approval became a soldier again for three weeks, this time with a uniformed wife by his side. By his side, but not in his bed. We slept four women or men to a room in bunk beds. I did not look forward to that arrangement, but good soldiers march onward. As it turned out, we met another future soldier, Judy Haber, as we boarded our flight from San Francisco. She was likable and

 enthusiastic, and I was happy that she agreed to be one of my bunkmates. The friendship we formed with this contemporary of Lynn's has spanned the next four decades.

Volunteers for Israel, 1988; Judy Haber far left

I really had no idea what was awaiting us, but we were about to be part of a rewarding adventure that permitted us to experience Israeli life in a way that could not have happened on any other kind of trip. A delightful Sar-El (the Israeli name for this program) coordinator greeted us at the Ben Gurion Airport and whisked us off to an army supply base close to the Sea of Galilee. We were shown our quarters, donned our khakis and army boots, and were given choices of tasks we could perform in coordination with the soldiers on the base, who welcomed us with open arms. A wonderful woman from Kansas, Ester Rudnick, and I chose to test the functionality of tank helmet wires that connected to the wires in the tank when the vehicle went into action. Ernie, forever the sculptor, decided to operate the machine that removed rust from metal to make the item reusable again; and our new friend Judy was often seen on the forklift in the warehouse.

Ester and I worked with two pleasant young soldiers who had immigrated to Israel from Morocco and Iraq with their families and were now serving their two years of mandated service in the Israeli Defense Force. They were stunned by the diligence with which we performed our tasks. Why did we never take a break? All the volunteers and soldiers were delighted to work together, and we had been told that the example we set by our work ethic might have a

Testing helmets: Liesel, Ester Rudnick

positive influence on those with whom we would be working. We may not have accomplished very much during these three weeks but living among Israelis opened our eyes to the fact that the army does everything it can to keep the country safe.

The entire trip was unforgettable, but what I am about to describe left an indelible mark on my understanding of how this little nation functions successfully, despite the problems it still must overcome.

Not only did the army welcome us volunteers, but we also were given a choice of where and with whom we would like to spend our two-day weekends. Israeli families opened their homes to volunteers who wanted to spend the weekends amidst their families. We inadvertently made a wonderful choice to spend the first weekend with Ruthie and Colonel Motte Dvir and family in the charming community of Kfar Tavor, located in the foothills of Mount Tabor. Upon our arrival, we received a warm but brief welcome from our hostess, who showed us where to deposit our luggage and then asked us to help with preparations for one of the children's birthday parties. We were not treated as guests but participated in all the activities of the household of a family with three active children—and we loved it.

The Dvirs did much more than host us for the weekend. When they realized that Ernie and I were keenly interested in the life of their community, they tried to expose us to others who lived within twenty-five miles from Kfar Tavor. Colonel Motte took us to visit his loyal batman, an Israeli Circassian who lived in a Circassian community approximately fifteen miles to the north. Their ancestors were Sunni Muslims who had to escape from the Russian Caucasus region in 1876 and fled to the then-Ottoman Empire, which settled these experienced fighters in what is now known as the Israeli Galilee. Their customs and religious practices differed from the local Shiite Muslims and they were sympathetic to the Jewish presence in Israel.

Ruthie took us to visit her mother, a Holocaust survivor who lived on a kibbutz near to Kfar Tavor, which had also been Ruthie's home until she married Motti. The Dvirs were on exceptionally good terms with a Bedouin Knesset member who lived in a Bedouin village no more 500 feet from their house on the hillside of Mount Tabor, and all four of us were invited to have dinner at their house. The food was wonderful and the sparkling conversation so interesting. If you walked out to the meadow behind the Dvirs' house and looked toward the right, you could see Nazareth in the distance, whose population today is 69 percent Shiite Arabs and 31 percent Israeli Christians. To me, this demonstrated that these diverse groups living within a 25-mile radius put their differences on the back burner to live in peace and harmony with their neighbors.

We spent the second weekend in Haifa with distant cousins. These good people fled to Chile in 1940 but moved to Israel when that country was created in 1948. As I had never been surrounded by a large extended family, it was a pleasure to be in the presence of Heinz and Inge Angress and her mother, my father's contemporary, who could describe what my dad had been like as a little boy. Our dear friend Ernie Hirscheimer's sister Barbara had also moved to Haifa when she married Czech-born Menachim Golan. This hospitable, bright, active couple was engaged in supporting a cause to recognize the West Bank as part of the Palestinian State, a point of view that was unthinkable to our American and Canadian Jewish friends. The inequities of this situation have always disturbed me. However, before I could consider joining the Golans' cause, I would need to be assured that the Palestinians would stop teaching their children to hate Jews and stop promoting the idea that the Jews should be driven off the land into the sea.

We chose to spend the third and last weekend with an Orthodox couple and their three children, whose views were in direct opposition politically to the Golans'. They put down their roots in Ma'le Adumim, an ultramodern settlement town in the West Bank that abuts Jerusalem and houses 40,000 people today, and whose development has been debated not only in Israel but worldwide. We thoroughly enjoyed our stay with the vibrant Etti and Avi Golam and felt enriched by the opportunity to experience the distinct aspects of Israeli life.

A few more days of work awaited us at the base, but Ernie and I were given time off to personally plant two trees we bought from the Jewish National Fund to add to the other four that had been planted

Ernie & Liesel plant trees, 1987

in our name, among the millions. The eighth day of Chanukah that year was celebrated before we were to leave Israel. Ruthie and Motti invited us back to Kfar Tavor to celebrate this night with them, forty-five members of their large extended family, and friends. Because Israel is small, large numbers can gather with the greatest of ease. Ruthie had initiated a tradition in the candle-lighting ceremony. Each of the eight candles commemorated an important event or achievement, and our work as volunteers was celebrated with one of the candles. We were touched to be honored by these wonderful people who had become our good friends.

Of course, there was also a farewell party to attend at the base. We were not only loathe to say goodbye to the soldiers who helped to make our stay so enjoyable, but it also was hard to part from fellow volunteers with whom we had experienced these wonderful three weeks. It should be noted that my husband may have been a trendsetter in demanding that he be allowed to serve at the age of seventy. Today, thousands of people still volunteer their time and there does not seem be an age limit anymore. A ninety-year-old whose doctor has verified that he is in good health is welcome in this wonderful program. I believe Ernie would join me in telling you how important this trip was for both of us. We had traveled a great deal, and now realized that interacting with the citizens of a country makes a trip much more meaningful than merely visiting the important sights recommended by a tour director or guidebook.

In 1999, after I was widowed, I traveled to eight countries with a company called Overseas Adventures. Those trips, with a maximum of sixteen fellow travelers, always included interactions with the citizens of the country. In Japan, for example, our hosts opened their homes to three people in our group. My hostess showed us how to dress ourselves in complicated, beautiful kimonos and how to perform the tea ceremony. On another day we learned to make sushi but were first taken to a nearby farm to pick the ingredients ourselves. Compared with the names and locations of beautiful Shinto shrines, these personal interactions are unforgettable.

Liesel in traditional kimono

In retrospect, 1988 seems like the calm before the storm. Before I describe the dramatic events that occurred in the following years, I want to tell you how I joined the modern world of computer users. Our little synagogue, Temple Beth El, had moved to a large modern building that could accommodate its growing membership. Innovative programs were planned, and one of them was to invite an eminent lecturer to speak at a two-day, scholar-in-resident event. As I had experience scheduling lecturers from my job at our Montreal synagogue, I offered to chair two of these events with the help of a capable committee, of which the kind David Rigler was a member. David offered to print the programs on his computer.

He invited me to the home that he and his wife Marilyn, an active community member, had built overlooking a typical California canyon, where this miraculous machine was located.

I was stunned and intrigued by his skills and the ease with which he operated this modern invention and decided there and then to buy my first Dell laptop and join the computer revolution. All the Kraz men have been at my disposal ever since, to help me operate and keep it functional. The Word program I use to draft this story is a godsend, as is the information I can retrieve on Google to assure myself that historical facts are correct. I do not need to pick up heavy encyclopedias or consult my ten-pound dictionary, which at my stage of life would be burdensome. My communication on email keeps me in touch with more people than I could write to by putting a pen on paper.

I wish there was no Twitter, and I have not joined Facebook or any other social media platform. I believe these media limit human interaction in real time and are a detriment to a factual, ordered world. Yet, the fact that I have become proficient enough to shop for necessities, partake in Zoom gatherings and play duplicate bridge online, especially during the 2020 pandemic, has been a great asset. Although I have never become as computer savvy as my late friend David, I am forever grateful to him. He made me aware that learning to use a computer would allow me to participate more fully in today's electronic world.

Bookshop Santa Cruz after 1989 earthquake

Chapter Thirteen
Paradise Crumbling

WE KNEW, WHEN we settled in Santa Cruz, that we were settling over the San Andreas Fault, where large masses of earth move past each other at 26mm annually. We also knew, as with tectonic plates all over the world, that greater movement might occur, potentially harming our otherwise calm existence in paradise.

Small quakes occurred annually that caused little concern, but strong foreshocks in the fall of 1988 and summer of 1989 had seismologists genuinely concerned as to what might be in store for us. Unconcerned, Ernie and I visited our niece Carla in Washington, DC, where we were eager to explore all the Smithsonian exhibits. Around 10:00 pm on the evening of October 17, 1989, Carla called us at the hotel and told us to turn on the TV to see what was happening in Santa Cruz and throughout the Bay Area. We were extremely fortunate to be able to reach the Issenmans, who assured us that our house was still standing—although minus its brick chimney and with broken china. We were so relieved that this large quake (6.9 on the Richter scale), which left so much destruction in its wake, inflicted comparatively minor damage on us.

The quake was responsible for sixty-three deaths and 3,757 injuries, and toppled numerous structures in the Bay Area. Six of the sixty-three deaths occurred in Santa Cruz County; downtown Santa Cruz was decimated. The Cooper House, an 1894 brick landmark, had been a popular gathering spot and now sadly needed to be demolished. Its cafés and music venues were missed by all who gathered there to listen and make music, including Ernie and other

Santa Cruz music lovers. Everyone who experienced the earthquake remembers every detail of the moment it struck. Having been absent, we felt left out when the subject was discussed. Although we shared the numerous aftershocks with neighbors and friends, we did not have the experience of watching chimneys falling, groceries toppling off shelves, or the asphalt moving in waves across a parking lot.

We did, however, participate in a memorable effort to save Bookshop Santa Cruz, owned by our friends, Neal and Candy Coonerty. The bookshop was housed in a multistory building where the new books were displayed on the street level and the used books and offices were on the lower floor. A wall had fallen at the side of both levels, and it was considered dangerous to enter either floor. Neal and Candy were so anxious to save their livelihood that they asked the authorities to consider installing supports to stop the wall from collapsing so they, with the help of volunteers, could remove the books. They received permission to achieve the task in two days. This city treasured its bookshop. Each of the 400 volunteers signed a waver, donned a hardhat, and came to carry the books to safety and store them in boxes that were loaded onto trucks that miraculously appeared on the scene. Some time later, tents were erected, and it took three years before a new, safe venue could be found. Rebuilding downtown Santa Cruz with strong, retrofitted, earthquake-resistant buildings took years, more than thirty to build the first seven-story multifunctional building on the lot that once housed the bookshop.

At our home, as anything made of brick was in danger when an earthquake struck, we rebuilt our chimney of material that could withstand another. We also had our garage and large deck retrofitted to ward off future damage.

With more than 100 aftershocks recorded, the entire population was in a constant state of anxiety but, very slowly, life returned to a new normal. Yes, earthquakes will happen, but not every year or even every few years or decades. Today, thirty-three years later, there are very few people living near the San Andreas Fault who give even a moment's thought to that possibility.

On Ernie's seventy-second birthday, November 9, not even a month after the earthquake, another important event took place. On that day, the Berlin Wall fell. It had been erected in 1961 to stop the multitude of Germans who lived in Soviet-controlled East Germany from escaping to the West. This was not a major event for my fellow Santa Cruzans, but it was an extremely important event for all German citizens and foreshadowed the collapse of the Soviet Union which, since the 1948 peace agreement after WW II, had control of the Eastern European countries. In researching to accurately describe this event, I learned that when the wall came down, confusing government directives allowed thousands to pour into West Berlin from the East. Decisions at various checkpoints were made independently, including one checkpoint manned by an officer who had worked at the border for thirty years and believed he was dying of cancer. He felt he had nothing to lose when he made the crucial decision to open the gates that would unite Germany and its capital.

The significance of this event for me goes back to 1948, when all German Jews who had lived in the Western zone could either receive compensation for their losses or return to Germany and reclaim their properties. Those of us who escaped the Nazi regime from what became the Soviet-controlled Eastern zone did not have those opportunities. The destruction of the Wall and the unrest in all the Russian satellite countries gave us hope that when the Soviet Union relinquished control, East and West Germany would unite, and we would be able to reclaim what had been taken from us in the 1930s.

And that is exactly what happened in 1990.

The Cold War, a global power struggle between dictatorship and democracy, ended in Berlin in 1989. Less than a year later, on October 3, 1990, East and West Germany were once again unified, but that historical event was possible only with the consent of the WW ll Western allies and communist Soviet Union. The concessions made by Mikhail Gorbachev, a Soviet reformer who came to power in 1985, were key to that agreement. He recognized that his own country needed change and that his policies of *glasnost* (openness) and *perestroika* (reform) would improve conditions for the Russian population. At the same time, he stated, "No matter what happens to our socialist brother countries, these states are responsible for themselves."

Gorbachev's decision not to march into Poland, Hungary, and East Germany in 1990 was a decidedly different approach from decades past, when calls for democratic freedom had been brutally crushed. My brother and I, our cousins in South America, and all our acquaintances who had the possibility of reclaiming what they had left behind in the 1930s, retrieved the documents of ownership from their archives—if they had been lucky enough to escape with them. Having taken possession, upon my father's death, of all the papers of our emigration, I had all the information required to start this process of restitution.

My brother Fred and I hired a lawyer in New York who collaborated with a lawyer in Dresden to achieve our goal of being reimbursed for the loss of two large homes and the 1933 state-of-the-art glove factory in Chemnitz, as well as a smaller one in the adjacent town of Jansdorf. The Beckers also owned another small property that we did not deem important, but that turned out to be a bigger windfall than we ever could have hoped for. The process was long and arduous not only because of legal complexities, but also because the number of heirs had increased over the years and all their information needed to be documented, to distribute whatever amount was realized proportionately. Of course, we were anxious to see which properties were still intact, but a trip to Chemnitz was not in the cards until several years later.

Our reaction to the earthquake was to repair the damage and prepare our home for the next one and, when the Iron Curtain was lifted, we saw an opportunity to regain what had been lost. But responding to an Alzheimer's diagnosis, a disease for which there is no cure, proved to be the greatest challenge. In 1981, when Ernie was sixty-four, he had registered for a memory course (which the instructor forgot to attend!). From then until 1990, this astute, literate, artistic man found himself becoming more forgetful and was often greatly frustrated at his waning ability to balance financial statements, compose a letter, or complete his latest sculpture. Fortunately, Ernie was in excellent health, and he and his friend Bernie worked out regularly at the local spa. On one fateful visit to the gym, however, he exercised well beyond his need or capability, collapsed, and was taken to the hospital. Despite having been declared to be well, this incident revealed a lack of judgment that was more worrisome than the other symptoms.

Although we wanted to attribute his decline to the normal aging process, at the same time we were fully aware of the possibility that Ernie had progressive Alzheimer's disease. During his diagnosis, his responses were judged to be below average, but the telling indicator that this fine man had Alzheimer's was the fact that he had lost the ability to distinguish between the little and the big hand on the face of a clock and could not tell the time. The diagnosis did not come as a shock to either of us. I remember clearly, as we descended the steps from the doctor's office and stood for a minute hugging each other, that we decided at that moment this was not going to destroy our lives, nor were we going to deny to anyone that these disabilities were now part of his being. He did not have to pretend that they did not exist.

At the doctor's office we were made aware of a study of acetyl-l-carnitine, a drug thought to be of benefit for Alzheimer's patients. It was taking place at Stanford University, and they were hoping to be able to register more of those afflicted with the disease. We registered Ernie very soon after the diagnosis and both felt that we were taking initiative—taking steps not only to help Ernie but others as well.

After approximately six months, the study was terminated. They were unable to recruit an adequate number of patients and, even for those who had participated, there was no evidence that acetyl-l-carnitine improved their symptoms. The most beneficial part of the study proved to be our sessions with an extremely bright and caring psychiatric nurse whom we met with throughout the study. She approved of the decision Ernie and I had made on the steps of the neurologist's office and gave us confidence that we were managing this sad news in the most positive manner.

During this period, Ernie continued his regular activities. He had a wonderful voice and sang in the temple choir; we continued to attend rehearsals of the San Francisco Symphony with our friends, and often stayed overnight with our new friend from Volunteers for Israel, Judy Haber. At the gym, he was supervised so that he would not exercise beyond his capabilities. He continued to tend the protea at the Arboretum and perhaps it was there, overlooking the waters of Monterey Bay, that he formulated a plan for another adventure.

Ernie had always loved to sail, and now expressed a desire to cross the Atlantic aboard a merchant vessel. He also mapped out another trip after landing in Europe: to the Dordogne in France to see the 25,000-year-old cave drawings; to watch geese being force fed—a horrible procedure—so that the French could have their foie gras; and to visit Rocamadour, a city carved out of a mountain. Was this wise? It was out of the question for me to accompany him on the ocean voyage because I would be sick the entire journey, due to my inner ear problem. But could we help him to navigate the hurdles of getting onboard and off board safely? I could make sure that he boarded the right plane to Boston where our good friend Bernice Godine, the wife of Ernie's best man, would see to it that he boarded the right vessel. In the meantime, I would fly to Europe, spend a week with my former Dutch schoolmates, and await the sailor when the vessel docked in Antwerp.

We completed those plans without a hitch.

Confronted with the hopelessness of Alzheimer's disease, we still wanted to try anything that might stop the deterioration of his brain. It was not a professional but a layperson who told us of a German homeopath who had successfully administered a series of injections that had helped a friend of theirs. I contacted the lady, who practiced her profession in a rural area between Frankfurt and Kaiserslautern in Germany. She suggested that we plan to spend a month in the area so she could give Ernie the required number of injections.

We rented a guest house on a farm near her office and, with our daughter Lynn in tow, made our trip to Germany. I had trepidations about returning to the country that in the 1930s and '40s could not tolerate my Jewish presence, but unlike many of my compatriots, I did not hold the entire German population responsible for the terrors of those years. I was unsure,

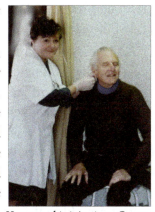

Homeopathic injections, Germany

however, how I would react to meeting an older person who might have participated in the horrors visited upon the Jews of Germany and neighboring nations.

Our landlady did not greet us with open arms. When she inquired where I had learned to speak German so well, I responded: "I was born in Germany, but being Jewish was forced to escape the Nazi menace." Since there was no reaction or response to that statement, I wondered how welcome we really were. My Lynn was surprised and

taken aback to hear me say this to anyone who asked me that question. But as time went on, I would hear her echo my explanation whenever she could. Why did I have the need to be so forthright? It is not something I had planned, but it was the only way I could interact with the German people at that point in time, and nobody

Landlady, Germany seemed disturbed by my honesty.

Our landlady astonished me greatly when she came one day to ask whether I would like to accompany her to the small plot of Jewish graves she looked after. I was pleased to drive with her through large farms to a small fenced-in gravesite where less than a dozen well-preserved graves were located. She explained that Germany was committed to looking after Jewish cemeteries after the war. My concern about her anti-Semitism evaporated and I thanked her for contributing to help to heal old wounds, but never questioned her decision to preserve Jewish cemeteries or how she funded the expense of doing so.

As I was writing this, my curiosity was aroused, as the Jewish cemetery in my hometown of Chemnitz was also well looked after. Google steered me in the right direction to find the answers I sought. The credit must be given to one of the successful Nuremberg Nazi trial judges, the time-honored Benjamin B. Ferencz. By virtue of the US Military Government restitution law, the Jewish Restitution Successor Organization (JRSO) became the lawful title holder of all Jewish cemeteries. At the time in 1949, Ferencz was only twenty-seven years old, but in later years he authored an article entitled "Reclaiming Cemeteries." The article explains his involvement in making Germany responsible for all the upkeep, in perpetuity, of hundreds Jewish cemeteries, as the congregations that cared for them had been destroyed and the ancestors of the deceased had been eliminated or forced to emigrate. He wrote, "Little did I realize what lay in store, if I may use such terminology. First, it was essential to learn precisely what was permissible or impermissible regarding the ancient burial grounds for religious organizations that no longer existed. It was not something taught in my property class at Harvard as, unfortunately, the Talmud was not assigned reading."

For those very reasons, he managed to engage the help of three distinguished rabbinic scholars to advise him on religious practices and prohibitions concerning such holy plots. Jewish laws dictate that once a cemetery, always a cemetery; no flowers can be placed on the casket or the grave; if a tombstone falls, it must be left lying where it fell, and more. The German committee, led by a Mr. Katzenstein, agreed only to cut the grass around the Jewish gravesites for the next twenty years, but not in perpetuity. They explained that they could not burden German taxpayers to assume an indefinite burden for Jews that they did not even give to their own German citizens. Ferencz wrote, "That did it. I exploded. The wrath of Ferencz was upon them. I shouted at them that if they had not murdered the Jews and driven them out, they would not have any problem with Jewish cemeteries."

Katzenstein ran from the room and a recess was called. Twenty minutes later, when the parties reassembled, the German representatives quietly said they would accept the obligation to honor the Jewish traditions. This meant that former Jewish cemeteries would be cared for and maintained at German government's expense forever, and that is why my landlady was given financial support to perform the task of looking after the nine graves we visited together. According to statistics, in 1949 only 29 percent of the German population supported this decision, but it was later applauded by a larger percentage of the younger generation, who recognized the harm done by their elders.

During our month in Germany, my Ernie received his allotted number of homeopathic injections, but that did not prevent us from traveling in a northerly direction to explore Mainz and Frankfurt and visit Martin Luther's Worms, which at one time housed a large, vibrant Orthodox Jewish community dating back to the eleventh century. The oldest grave has 1059 engraved on its gravestone. Knowing what I know now about German Jewish cemeteries, I should not have been surprised at how well the more than 4,000 graves were kept.

Lynn had expressed that she wanted to visit Dachau, the earliest concentration camp built in 1933, only sixteen kilometers north of Munich. We set off in a southerly direction on the Autobahn with her driving our rental car. As there were no speed limits on certain stretches of that highway, our daughter threw caution to the wind and took her parents for an unforgettable ride at 110 kilometers per hour. We arrived very quickly in Heidelberg, where we wanted to see the oldest still-functional university, established in 1356. Our next stop was Rothenberg, founded in 1274 and famous for its medieval architecture. From there we went on to Augsburg, the third oldest city in Germany, founded by the Romans in 15 BC. This German-born girl's knowledge of German history began with WW I; the only other scant information I had about the German political structure I gleaned from the programs of concerts I attended. German composers' benefactors were the German princes who ruled small municipalities. I knew more about Austrian, French, and Italian history because I had visited those countries frequently; but now, as we passed through these ancient cities, I became aware of Germany's long, interesting past.

When we entered the city of Dachau, we asked a police officer to give us directions to the camp. The proud man gave us the directions but insisted there were other worthwhile sights to see in Dachau, obviously unhappy that the camp had become his home's main attraction. As we approached the entrance to the camp, we were pleased to watch a large group of German students leaving. The Germans were not sweeping their past under the rug; it was an open book and every West German had to study it.

The day after writing this last sentence, I went to San Francisco with seven of my dear Christian friends, ages 75–85, who are art lovers. We went to view an exhibit of the unearthed treasures of Pompeii. I decided to do a survey and ask what the name Dachau meant to them. To my great surprise, all but one knew of the horrors that happened there, and two had visited the site while living several years in Munich.

I only recently learned that 150 camps scattered throughout southern Austria and Germany were collectively called Dachau. Although it does not nearly convey the enormity of what happened

Dachau gate

during those years as does Auschwitz (which I visited in 2005), the memorial at Yad Vashem, or the Holocaust Memorial Museum in Washington, Dachau is so important. It was the model for other concentration camps built throughout the rest of Germany, Poland, and the Czech Republic to imprison, torture and eventually kill political dissidents, including Catholic priests, Gypsies, gay people, the mentally disturbed, and eventually, six million Jews. Only the deceptive greeting as you enter, "*Arbeit Macht Frei*" meaning "Work shall set you free," the bunks where prisoners were housed, and a small museum recalling the events of its history remain at the camp in Dachau near Munich.

I did not look forward to our overnight in Munich because the specter of Hitler remained in my mind. However, I was quickly charmed by the beautiful architecture, parks, and beer gardens where we joined the local population to drink our share of beer and satisfy our hunger with bratwurst, sauerkraut and spaetzle. It rained heavily on the way back to our rental and I purchased a sturdy, colorful umbrella in Kaiserslautern, which I would later learn was my paternal grandfather's birthplace. I still use it today and it brings back memories of the sadly unsuccessful attempt we made to try to help my Alzheimer's-afflicted husband.

We had one more stop before boarding our flight for home. We wanted to take Lynn to Bloemendaal and reconnect with my childhood friends. Lily, the organizer, had gathered Tinneke, Hanneke and their husbands for a delicious light luncheon in the home that she had inherited, where I used to play. Lynn could not get over the camaraderie that existed among us and the joy we felt in reuniting.

Holland friends: Liesel, Hanneke, Lynn, Tinneke & spouses

As we all dined in Zandvoort on the North Sea, someone I did not recognize touched me on the shoulders and exclaimed, "It is really you, Liesel?" This former classmate then explained she heard I was visiting and just had to see the girl who disappeared so suddenly without any explanation in 1939. Yes, I was so fortunate to escape Europe just in time, but I will always remember the wonderful years I spent, from age six to thirteen, among such good people who remained friends throughout my life.

Ernie & Liesel, Jewish Museum, Germany

Chapter Fourteen
Losing Ernie

WHEN OUR HOUSE caught fire in 1992, it was entirely our fault.

We were not there to watch our bedroom, kitchen and bathroom go up in smoke since we had departed again, this time to visit Ruth and Edgar Cohen at their summer retreat in Old Orchard Beach. We had prepared the house for the painters in our absence and Ernie had wired the lamps in our bedroom to go on at night to deter burglars from assuming they would be welcome. I wanted the lamps to be on the beds to avoid having the painters knock them over accidentally in our absence.

Well, you can figure out what happened.

We motored happily up the coast of Massachusetts and Maine, visiting friends, eating our fill of wonderful Maine lobster, and even reluctantly entering antique shops, although we had agreed never to acquire another thing. Nonetheless, we found two lovely wooden folding chairs that would come in handy for our visitors. Ruth and Edgar welcomed us and insisted that before we do anything else, we had to sit down and have a drink. Of course, the liquor was intended to calm our nerves before they gave us the shocking news. Bernie Issenman had called to let us know that a fire had caused substantial damage to our house.

We shipped the two chairs home and flew back to a house that would not be our home for the next four months. Our insurance agent was a gem. His efficiency gave us little time to reflect on our loss. He told us that the house had to be emptied of all its belongings after an insurance adjuster had looked at the damage, and that we and the fire damage restoration company had to make a list of everything that was removed. He had an efficient contractor standing ready to begin work on the reconstruction.

Again, we liked our house and were not moving walls, but since we needed new bathroom fixtures, we got a deeper bathtub that could cover me entirely with soap bubbles, and since we could now afford a new kitchen (due to the remarkably high valuation of an ancient carpet under our bed), I chose a pricey pale peach art deco design that I am still in love with. A picture in a magazine convinced us that the art deco design of a large headboard with night tables and attached bookcase with a floating support for a mattress would also suit us perfectly. Choosing knobs for kitchen cupboards and drawers can be mind-numbing. Finding the right bathroom fixtures took time and selecting the wallpaper for both the kitchen and bathroom was an ordeal. None of it was simple, but the people we dealt with were most cooperative.

Though the fire was a shocking experience, I realized that it gave me the opportunity to be creative and that all the problems we had to overcome were challenges we were able to handle. Thirty years later, I still am delighted with what we created.

Gil & Mimi Stein

During all of this, we were still at the beginning of Ernie's slow deterioration. Once we realized that the homeopathic injections did not improve his condition, we gave up looking for cures and continued instead with all our activities, enjoying interactions with our old friends and some new ones—all of whom were so supportive during this prolonged, challenging time and would eventually become the bedrock of my existence after I lost Ernie.

Through our association with the Israeli Study Group of Temple Beth El, we befriended the much younger Mimi and Gil Stein. Mimi shares the immigrant experience with me. She was born in Morocco to parents who allowed her to join a group of thirty Jewish children who were shepherded to

Israel to live a fruitful existence among its people. She became a nurse and met Gil, an American lawyer, who was drawn to the experience of kibbutz life in Israel. They married and eventually came to Santa Cruz with their two boys.

A member of my book group suggested that I welcome the Canadian-born newcomer Miriam Fishman and her husband, Noel, to Santa Cruz. I am so glad that I got to meet this exceptionally fine couple. We became close friends, although they eventually moved to warmer San Diego to be closer to family. The battery on my phone often becomes depleted when we bring each other up to date on all that is new in our lives.

Dr. Harold Gordon, a WW II veteran like Ernie, moved to Santa Cruz with his wife Annie to live out their lives near their daughter, Margaret. These delightful people found us through an East Coast connection and joined the Issenmans and us for a monthly brunch, which we all looked forward to. Interacting with these bright people was so stimulating. If you live long enough, you must make new friends constantly. I have been fortunate to be able to do that as the old ones depart for what my Christian friends call "home."

But all was not easy. Over the next few years, Ernie experienced two difficult rejections because of his Alzheimer's disease. It came as a shock to me when Temple Beth El engaged a UCSC music professor to direct their choir who insisted that every participant be able to read music. My music-loving husband was no longer able to do that and was dismissed. The fact that his participation was a form of therapy was never considered; the perfection of the choir's performance was what mattered. I blame myself for not being more assertive and letting this decision pass, but it is unfortunate that a house of worship showed little concern for a person who needed support.

This incident and the desire to be a part of a more conservative congregation like the one in which we grew up led us to join other members of the Israeli Study Group, like the Fishmans, in the newly formed Congregation Kol Tefillah. As a small group, services were conducted by knowledgeable members, since hiring a rabbi was not affordable.

The second rejection is one that most people find difficult to deal with. One of Ernie's doctors thought it would be better if he did not drive any more. He fought like a veritable tiger to have that decision overturned and demanded to be interviewed by a DMV controller to prove that he was still capable of operating a vehicle safely. Amazingly, he was successful—but not for long. Six months later he lost his license. I do not believe that Ernie ever had a car accident or received a citation, even though, for forty-five years, I often felt fearful and loudly expressed my apprehensions while sitting next to him in the passenger seat. Our children decided that this was the one cause of disagreement in our marriage.

When behind the wheel, this otherwise rational man had no patience to drive behind a slower vehicle on a two-lane highway and constantly considered passing the slower car at an unlikely speed. He also took it as a personal affront when a red light stopped

Alex & Ernie

him in his tracks. Therefore, I, too, felt that the disease which was altering his brain might affect his sometimes-questionable driving behavior. Of course he was upset, but to prove he was still independent, he decided to use the complicated Santa Cruz transit system. Instead of a ten- to fifteen-minute car ride, it took him an hour and a quarter to get to the gym and the same stretch of time to return.

At this point we hired a quiet, nice young man, a nursing student at Cabrillo College. Alex would eventually move into a bedroom on our lower floor with its own entrance. We provided him with a little fridge, a microwave and toaster oven, as well as access to the kitchen when he needed it. At first, he assisted in getting Ernie to his activities, but as time progressed and I could not leave Ernie unsupervised at home, Alex's presence allowed me to continue playing golf and duplicate bridge in the company of friends, giving me the respite I needed as a caregiver.

But before all of this, the travel-addicted Sabloffs took another trip to Israel with the Elderhostel travel company in 1992. We enjoyed a week of lectures on social studies at Tel Aviv University, including field trips; another week studying anthropology at the University of Haifa; and a third week at the University of Jerusalem studying archaeology. The student in Ernie happily listened attentively even though he could not absorb the information.

In 1994, we rented a spacious home in Provence for a month. Our daughter Nancy accompanied us on this journey, which she claims was the best of her life. She has given me permission to share some of the entries in her diary with you.

Liesel, Ernie and I arrived in France on April 30, rented a car and drove around the entire perimeter of Paris; the traffic was so heavy it made Los Angeles look like heaven on earth. Dad was grumpy after having been trapped in a plane, boxed in like a sardine.

Ernie, Nancy & Singing Heads

We finally escaped the traffic, stopped at the town of Chorey-les-Beaune, and toured the petit village after having taken a nap. We came upon a sizable castle surrounded by a moat. It was such a tremendous change from the hustle-bustle of the modern world to arrive at an ancient structure surrounded by plant life. There were flowers everywhere—forget-me-nots, comfrey, watercress, iris, wisteria and lilacs.

The second day of travel we chanced upon a charming arts and crafts fair. Most impressive were the giant ceramic heads with musical sounds coming from their mouths. I have a photo of the father I adore and myself singing along with the sculptures.

We arrived at the village of Saint-Siffret, our home for a month, 20 km east of Avignon and close to the town Uzès. It is an ancient place with stone paths winding throughout and a road barely accessible for one car. We were utterly charmed. Our home was a three-story abode completely outfitted for all our needs. It had a balcony that looked over a beautiful valley full of cherry orchards where swallows swooped and dove at sunset. It felt like we had gone back to much simpler times.

My daughter continued to write page after page extolling the food we bought at the markets, the beautiful towns perched on hilltops we visited, the Roman structures that were still intact such as the magnificent enormous Pont du Gard, and how wonderful it was to have my lifelong friend, Liesel Gotch, join us for one week, and Judy Haber for another.

She also noted that her dad's inner time clock was damaged. On every journey we took, he felt we should have arrived at our destination 15–20 minutes after we had left home. On the very last trip we took, to celebrate my mother's ninety-fifth birthday in January of 1996, he insisted that it was time to get off the plane when we had just departed from San Jose and the seatbelt sign had been turned off. He was still strong and

Lotte Becker's 95th birthday. L to R: Lotte (seated), Daniel, Nancy, Liesel, Lynn, Ernie, Fred, Jeanie (caregiver)

angrily confronted me to let him get up. It took some doing to calm him down.

Ernie's condition changed dramatically during that year. He was no longer able to volunteer at the UCSC Arboretum and his days of exercise, playing golf and tennis, ended. He had been an avid reader and was denied that pleasure as reading became difficult and absorbing information impossible. My proud, independent husband started to need help with dressing and his bathroom routine and, of course, his mind could not process anything that involved our financial concerns. He had always appreciated my cooking, but his taste buds were also altered and the meals I prepared were no longer to his liking.

I cannot recall if he watched television, but the one thing he did enjoy was listening to jazz; it would lift his spirits. He also derived pleasure from looking at the photo albums of our trips, which brought back such good memories. From the time he had been a law student, he liked to have me nearby while he studied, and now he wanted me with him every moment of the day. Although it was not easy leaving him in the care of Alex or other help, I was fortunate to be able to afford to hire help to relieve me, so I could pursue the activities that afforded me the time I needed to return to him refreshed and ready to take on the next problems we encountered.

One day, Ernie escaped into the dense woods behind our home. All our caring neighbors were alerted and fortunately he was found unharmed within an hour. But the next worrisome deficit made me wonder how much longer I could care for him. He became terribly upset one evening when I opened the door to our living room, loudly claiming that it was too dangerous to enter. It seems that some Alzheimer's patients experience this anxiety because they cannot process the reflections that illumination causes to appear on windows.

I realized it was time to look for a nursing home very shortly after that incident. I remember exactly where we were standing in our house, talking with a visiting friend, when my remarkable, loving husband said to me, "You go, Liesel, I'm bad." Somehow, he recognized that he might strike out and hurt me or others unwittingly. Did he realize that living at home had now become an untenable situation?

In searching for a facility that was as pleasant as possible, I found a rural home that housed people with mental problems. Ernie was there not even a week when he physically attacked another patient, escaped, and was brought home by the police. Unfortunately, I now had the extremely emotional task of finding a locked Alzheimer's unit in a nursing home near San Jose, which he entered without question or hesitation. I had to accept that he would never come home again.

I joined the gentleman who had recommended the facility and daily visited his entirely disabled wife, who had been in the home for five years. I drove across the Santa Cruz Mountains with him three times a week to see Ernie, who always greeted me with open arms even though he might have to drop the hand of a female patient who had attached herself to him, or he may have sought out that contact.

50th wedding anniversary

We celebrated our fiftieth wedding anniversary on May 22, 1997, in a private room of the nursing home surrounded by a few close friends, and we danced together for the last time at an outdoor party for the patients and their guests.

These relatively pleasant moments ended after several months, when the staff of the home reported that Ernie's behavior was becoming more aggressive and that he was spitting out the medication needed to ameliorate such behavior. If this continued, he could no longer stay at that facility. As he did not comply with their rules, he was sent to Stanford Hospital, where they restrained him and even hired a guard to protect the other patients from this man who had once fought to save others' lives. I cannot remember whether the doctors injected him with the medication he needed, but I do remember that he would not swallow the pills prescribed and refused the food offered him.

Ernie and I had both signed "Do No Resuscitate" documents. When the children and I visited him at Stanford, we expressed our support that, if he did not want to eat anymore, he should not be forced. His doctor was appalled and exclaimed that she could not go along with that decision since she worked to save lives. She likened it to the killings in the Holocaust death camps.

Fortunately, we found a nursing home that accepted my dangerous husband on probation. However, before he could be moved there, I was told that I had to become his legal conservator. I hired a lawyer who led me through this process, but to this day I do not understand why it had now become necessary rather than when I committed him to the first luxurious nursing home of my choice.

We moved him, now an altered man and thirty pounds lighter, to a very simple facility where he lived not even three weeks. His formerly twinkling blue eyes had lost their spark and he had no appetite whatsoever. His doctor at this facility was proud of me when I insisted that his Durable Power of Attorney was to be clipped to the outside of his file at the nurses' station and, more importantly, another copy clearly displayed on the door of his room. When Ernie developed the pneumonia that would cause his death, his wishes were complied with. He was not given oxygen, nor was he injected with lifesaving antibiotics.

Nancy and I learned of his death as we were driving across the Santa Cruz Mountains to visit him and, as often as I have crossed those mountains since, I always recall the moment I heard of my best friend and loving husband's passing.

Those who attended his small memorial service, including his two brothers, recall that the downpour of days was suddenly interrupted and the clouds parted to reveal a little bit of blue sky. The burial service took place at the small Jewish cemetery that Ernie loved, and he was interred under a young tree which is now a full-grown, beautiful umbrella over his grave and others'.

Ruth Issenman, our longtime friend, spoke beautifully at the memorial. When we considered what should be written on his gravestone, she suggested: "Here lies one of nature's gentlemen who lived his life with grace and joy." That is engraved on the footstone that fronts the grave, which is headed by a large, sculpted rock I believe the sculptor in Ernie would have liked.

Sitting shiva is part of our Jewish tradition. *Shiva* is derived from the Hebrew word *sheva*, which means seven, signifying the seven days of mourning. Its primary purpose is to provide a time for spiritual and emotional healing. Mourners come to comfort family and friends, join in saying the Mourner's Kaddish, and share their memories of the deceased. According to tradition, mourning is to be focused entirely on the departed. It certainly was, but there were very few tears, because we all felt that in death Ernie had been released from his troubled, altered condition.

Nonetheless, after all family members departed, the reality of being widowed and no longer needed by anyone landed painfully and I cried whenever Ernie came to mind, or when someone mentioned his name. Although I had already lived several years without his guidance and help and one year entirely without his presence, all kinds of questions suddenly entered my mind. Will I be safe living by myself? Should I move to an apartment? Can I oversee all financial matters competently?

Slowly I began to realize that I had already been tested and that I loved where I lived, surrounded by all the possessions that remind me daily of my past. I resolved to make a five-year contract with myself that I have already renewed four times—to live as long as I can in my home, where I am surrounded by wonderful neighbors such as the renowned portrait artist Jenny Welty, husband Phil and two daughters, Taylor and Hillary; Sandy and Charles Eldridge; Karen Berchtold; and Ruth and Bernie Issenman, who continued to be my anchors in California.

Chapter Fifteen
Restitution and Resolutions

GERMAN LAWYERS CONTINUE to try to connect Jewish property owners with unclaimed property for a fee equal to 15 percent of its value. In 2006, an attorney discovered a property in Leipzig which he claimed still belonged to my maternal grandparents. We assured him they had sold that to pay for their escape to Holland in 1938. Then in early 2021, ninety years after we had left Chemnitz, a lawyer from Berlin wrote to me that he had discovered $6000 in a bank account belonging to my late father. It was mine if I paid him 15 percent to release it from the Jewish Claims Conference through which all restitution funds are repaid. What can they find next?

When I had returned to Chemnitz in 1992, I was still not entirely certain how I would react, being in the land of my birth that had done such harm to my family. On my way to Chemnitz, I stopped in Berlin and had time to stroll down the Kurfürstendamm, the Champs-Élysées of Berlin, to arrive at a plaza with a huge bronze plaque at the entrance of the subway station listing the concentration camps, to remind all who walked by that they must never be forgotten. Somehow the sight of that

Placque of camp names, Germany

plaque allowed me to feel more at ease. I felt that Germany was doing its best to make amends for the horrors of those days.

More relaxed, I returned to Chemnitz (as my brother Fred would do in 1993) to learn that the house we were born in had been destroyed, the Karl Becker residence was intact but could not be taken over by us because it was occupied by a preschool, and

only an exceedingly small, dilapidated portion of the state-of-the-art factory of 1933 was still standing. The grandeur of the 1930s era was nowhere in evidence except at the Jewish Cemetery, to which I was led by Siegmund Rotstein, a leader of the small Jewish community in Chemnitz. The large marble wall with

Becker family graves

my family's graves needed repair, but evidence of its splendor and craftmanship was still apparent. My brother and I would eventually have it restored to its former beauty.

Mr. Rotstein enlightened me that he was a survivor of the Holocaust who had returned to Chemnitz when he was twenty to create a Jewish community there with fifty-six other survivors. They held services with a Torah scroll that had been rescued from the old synagogue that was burned in 1938. He described how the Chemnitz authorities had helped throughout the years so their small Jewish community could survive in their midst.

Restitution payments were not based on the condition of properties in 1992; nor were we to be reimbursed for the actual value they would have had at that time. The restitution laws stated that for the two homes and the factory building, we were to be paid three times the value they had in 1933. I had supplied the lawyers with statements my father passed on to me, which clearly described the substantial value of the factory's equipment and inventory, and we would have been happy to be repaid for those assets and the prescribed value of the properties.

But a windfall came our way.

A German trust company that held all Jewish assets had unlawfully sold the small property abutting the Chemnitz factory, which according to my father's notes was valued at $15.600 marks. It was sold by the trust for several million to a gas company that built a gas station on it. It took a three-year battle until they were finally convinced of the illegality of their actions, and we were awarded the amount they had collected from the sale.

My mother, who was ninety-four at the time, was heir to half the amount realized in 1994 and, upon the advice of her lawyer and accountant, decided to allow these funds to bypass her and go to Fred and me. We considered ourselves so fortunate and were forever grateful to be able to live our lives without any financial worries—if we invested our good fortune wisely.

Two-thirds of the Karl Becker estate were inherited by the heirs of my late Aunt Erna and were distributed to her South American relatives and to distant cousins in Europe. She also left 10 percent to both Fred and me.

We only had two regrets when these funds became available.

It would have been wonderful if my dad could have experienced the fruits of his and his relatives' labor returned to their families. The other regret was that one-third of the Karl Becker estate was to be paid to the family of a former Nazi officer, whose late sister Freda Becker had been married to Eduard. He was her heir. The incredulity of this disturbed our entire extended family immensely.

Ernie and I had always looked after our own investments, but now we felt that we needed a financial advisor to invest both our and our mother's holdings. We hired the knowledgeable Morgan White, owner of Woodside Asset Management, who administered our portfolios and became a trusted friend. I have, however, never relinquished the nest egg my dad gave me to administer. It continues to give me the opportunity to make small investments in what

I observe to be developing industries, such as Tesla or Costco, and keeps me interested in our changing economy.

After we laid Ernie to rest in January 1998 and I had come to terms with my widowhood, I looked forward to traveling to the far-off countries that had not been on my husband's agenda. It was time to go to South America to contact the family members who had successfully settled there after escaping Germany. However, before connecting with my relatives in Argentina, I decided first to book a ten-day trip to Peru to visit Machu Picchu, at the very top of my bucket list. The Overseas Adventure Travel company, which limited the number of people on each tour to sixteen, was my choice for travel not only to Peru, but to eight other countries over the next twenty years.

Armed with pills to help me tolerate the great heights of the Andes, I landed in Lima. As the plane taxied towards the airport, I could see a mountain that had hundreds of thousands of poor dwellings on it, where Peruvians who had escaped from more rural poverty lived with the hope of finding jobs in the city. I would see this sad sight in Brazil as well. From Lima we flew to Cusco where, upon arrival, we were served a tea with coca leaves known to help one adapt to its 11,115-foot elevation, and which left sixteen intoxicated tourists laughing hilariously on our way to our hotel. I enjoyed visiting all the different sights in the charming city of Cusco, but if I were to relate to you the interesting experiences in all countries I visited, I might not be able to finish this long tale before my demise. However, the remote city of Machu Picchu, 74 km from Cusco, was so breathtaking, it needs to be described.

To see Machu Picchu at the best possible time, we stayed one night just below this World Heritage Site and rose before sunrise to get our first view of the massive, awe-inspiring Imperial Inca city. It is surrounded by large mountains that stretch over five miles. More than 3,000 steps link 150 buildings built of massive stone blocks cut to fit together without mortar, so tightly that not even a blade of grass could get between them. The site impressed me so enormously that I enlarged one of my photographs and hung it on the wall above my computer for years thereafter. During the rest of my stay, I learned how Peruvians farm, and that certain crops only grow on specific heights; that most children in the mountainous area must scale one or two steep hills to walk to school; and that when we visited a village at 12,000 feet, I had to pop the pills to prevent from getting sick.

After leaving the tour in Peru for Buenos Aires, I made an overnight stop at the Iguazu Falls, which resemble an elongated horseshoe extending 1.7 miles, three times wider than Niagara Falls and significantly greater than the African Victoria Falls. I marveled at the natural beauty and ferocity of that collection of waterfalls that thunder into a river where Argentina and Brazil meet.

The purpose of my trip to Buenos Aires was to visit with the family of my father's late sister, Lily. They had escaped to Argentina in the late 1930s. Lily's son Werner, the nephew my father adored, had married a lady named Ruth, whose family were also immigrants. Like so many immigrants from different countries all over the world, they settled in a community with their own people. Unfortunately, Werner had passed away a few years prior to my visit, but I spent wonderful days in that beautiful city with his widow, Ruth, and in the company of Pedro, their youngest son, his wife and their two teenage children. The older son, Carlos, had married a Brazilian woman and I would spend time with them in Rio de Janeiro on the last segment of this trip.

I loved the rhythm of the tango, and Pedro took me to a club famous for observing experts dance in great style to that haunting music. Of course, I also had to see Eva Peron's famous tomb with an inscription she wrote herself that proclaims, "I will return. And I will be millions."

A minor inconvenience delayed my flight to Montevideo, Uruguay to meet with the cousins who had lived around the corner from me in Chemnitz. As a Canadian citizen, I needed a visa to enter that country that was not in my possession. Unbelievably, the Canadian embassy was open on Saturdays until 1:00 pm. I raced there by cab and got my visa in time to catch the next flight to meet with them, for tea rather than lunch.

The family I will now introduce shares a double set of genes with me. Their grandfather, Adolf Becker, was my grandfather Eduard's brother, and their grandmother, Flora, was my grandmother Lina's sister. Additionally, Flora and Adolf's daughter, Grete, was married to my Aunt Erna's brother, Kurt Bernstein, who were best friends of my parents. Their two daughters, Annie and Irene, were Fred's and my contemporaries; the tassel-haired, livewire Irene had been my first playmate in Chemnitz. The family had last visited us in Holland, and we had not encountered each other for sixty years.

When I arrived in Montevideo, those sixty years just melted away. Irene was still a livewire but, unlike my dyed mane, her hair was a natural mixture of brown and white. She and her husband Peter Gross, a bright, no-nonsense man, made me feel very welcome. They suggested I spend the next day visiting with Irene's sister Annie's family and then motor with them to Punta del Este, a resort town, for the rest of my stay. Unfortunately, my visit with Annie was brief. She herself was not in the best of health and the day I visited, her husband, Erich Kirscheimer, was extremely ill and hospitalized. She also had the ongoing concern of looking after her younger daughter, Diana, who had Down syndrome.

South American family

Annie's elder daughter, the lovely Sonia, was my companion throughout the rest of the day. We paid a brief visit to her father's bedside and then she proceeded to drive me around Montevideo, showing me the offices of Bernsen Limitada, the thriving business her grandfather and her father had built selling machinery and raw material, mainly cotton, which now fell to her to look after. Sonia is also the only one of all the South American offspring who continues to practice some Jewish traditions. She has also been an active member of an interfaith organization for years.

The following day, Irene and Peter picked me up to drive to their apartment in Punta del Este, where we spent three wonderful days reminiscing in beautiful surroundings. While we were there, the Gross children, Tony and Mario, came to visit with their wives, Tony's three strapping boys, and Mario's three daughters. Irene and Peter also have a daughter, Sylvia, who was married and lived in New York with her husband and two children. All three Gross children had attended the German school in Montevideo. Irene and Peter identified themselves as cultural Jewish atheists. They and their children never saw the inside of a synagogue in Montevideo and, like Pedro in Argentina and Carlos in Brazil, their three children all married spouses of other faiths.

However, their entire family does gather on Rosh Hashanah, the Jewish New Year, because Kurt Bernstein, their father and grandfather, left behind the request that they all be together twice a year, on the New Year and his birthday. I believe that if my children had ever considered marriage, they too would not have deemed it important to find a spouse of the same faith, though they graduated from our synagogue's Hebrew school and our son Daniel very competently recited his Hebrew bar mitzvah portion in front of the entire congregation.

While in Punta del Este, the Grosses took me to a gathering of their close friends and, to my amazement, they were all German Jewish immigrants like Irene, Peter, and myself. Sylvia recently told me that this tight group and their offspring remained the most important social contact for the Gross family throughout their lives. I was recently reminded by Sonia that I injected a little bit of Jewish tradition into their lives while in Uruguay by creating a Passover celebration at Mario's house, which she claims everyone greatly enjoyed. I left Uraguay for Brazil with a memento, a beautiful cowl-neck red sweater that Peter insisted on buying for me on one of our long walks in Punta del Este. Every time I wear it, it takes me back to those lovely days with my cousins.

Landing on a sunny day in Rio, I was met by affable, warmhearted Carlos Horwitz, who reminded me so much of the nephew my father loved. He had married the lovely Brazilian Portuguese-speaking Conchita, with whom unfortunately I could not converse, and they had two grown children—a son in his father's image, Carlos Werner, named for his father and grandfather, and a daughter who was in Germany while I visited.

I shall never forget how stunned I was when we approached Carlos's home; he pointed to a house built on a hillside and told me it was his, but kept driving only to return there five minutes later. Why did he do that? He responded that he wanted to be sure it was safe to enter his garage. To this day the answer does not make sense to me. However, I did learn that most people in this comparatively affluent neighborhood felt vulnerable to being robbed by the people who lived above them in a *favela* or slum, and often have guards outside their homes.

The Horwitz's home was within walking distance of the World Heritage botanical gardens and that is where Carlos, Carlos Werner and I spent a good part of the time during my visit. We also toured

the city and, upon my request, visited a spectacular modern saucer-like structure overhanging the water, designed by architect Oscar Niemeyer, which I had seen from the plane. The Horwitz men were such good hosts and Conchita

Niteroi Contemporary Art Museum   smilingly fed me her delicious Brazilian dishes. But the time had come to leave the South American continent for home. I was so happy to have become acquainted with all of them. It gave me a taste of what it might have been like to be surrounded by family, had we not been scattered in 1939.

I regret that I did not go to Colombia while on that continent to get acquainted with the Herrmanns, my mother's side of the family, but the civil conflict and drug trafficking stopped me from including that country on my itinerary. Fortunately, I had had occasion to meet three Herrmanns over the years. I had met the cute little Edith in Holland, the grandchild of Willi Herrmann, my grandmother's brother, and she came to live with us in Montreal for a year while attending university there. She was a joy to have around, but we never communicated after she returned to Bogotá to marry and raise a family. I also met the affable Ron Zander, another of Willi's grandchildren, when he appeared at a birthday celebration for Kurt Herrmann, my mother's younger cousin by seventeen years and the son of the late Harry and Rosa Herrmann.

The handsome young Kurt crossed my path frequently. I first encountered him when he paid us a visit in Holland. He, like all relatives who needed employment at that time, was still working for Gebrüder Becker in Chemnitz. In 1938, Kurt was dismissed from this now-Aryanized establishment and returned to his parents' home in Nordhausen. Shortly thereafter, he received an affidavit from my maternal grandfather's brother, Uncle Otto, stating that he would support Kurt financially once he received a visa to come to the United States.

There was no time to lose. Kurt bought a ticket to cross the Atlantic to Cuba, which had been welcoming Jews, but had to cancel that ticket when Cuba suddenly demanded a deposit of $5000 to one of their banks as a passage to freedom. Kurt kept the stub of that ticket in the suit he wore when he was taken to the Buchenwald concentration camp very shortly thereafter and where, for three weeks, he experienced all the horrors that have been related by other survivors. But luck was with this young man. For some reason, the Germans at that time agreed to let prisoners go if they had proof of a means to leave the country. Kurt presented them with the (cancelled) ticket in his pocket and his passport, and was free to go.

He knew that he had to find a way to leave Germany for Belgium, and described a harrowing trip with a knowledgeable smuggler who helped him cross that border to freedom. With the support of my parents, he lived in Belgium for the next six months until he finally got his American visa. Before departing from Europe, he visited his aunt, my grandmother Grete Frank, in Amsterdam, then crossed the Atlantic to begin the American part of his life.

In the United States, Kurt worked for several years, then in 1942 was invited to join the American forces because he could speak German. He was sent to Camp Ritchie, where he and 15,000 other German speakers, most of whom were Jewish immigrants, were trained as spies and interpreters to assist the American forces. Kurt

became a "Ritchie Boy" who proudly served under General Patton as they entered Germany at the end of the war. It is uncanny that, when I wrote about Benjamin Ferencz regarding the upkeep of the German Jewish graves, *60 Minutes* on CBS produced a program on all his works; and now, as I write about Ritchie Boys, CBS interviewed four survivors of that program and chronicled their importance to the US Army.

Kurt Herrmann

When he returned home, Kurt moved to Los Angeles and married Sue Grosz, an immigrant who had spent the war years in Shanghai. Their adored son, Robert, completed that family picture. This loyal cousin stayed in touch with my mother on a regular basis. Kurt and I would eventually share a great deal of Herrmann family history, which he was able to reconstruct with the help of the South African and Colombian branches of the family and archives from the city of Nordhausen.

Sue & Kurt Herrmann

But the most important document in my files today is a letter from the Jewish archives in Prague.

Kurt wrote to that organization to inquire if they had information about how and when his parents, Harry and Rosa Herrmann, and my grandmother, Grete Frank, had died. The response described their deaths in detail, with the dates and numbers of the transport that led to their extermination in Auschwitz. My cousin also provided me with copies of six, twenty-five-word Red Cross letters my grandmother wrote to her brother Willi in Colombia during the last years of her life in Amsterdam. Since we lived in Canada at that time and it was an enemy country, she could not send them to us. These letters, and the document revealing how she died, would travel with me to Auschwitz when I went to Poland in 2005.

My loyal cousin Kurt spent several delightful long weekends with me in Santa Cruz. I would visit him whenever I was in the Los Angeles neighborhood and attended all his milestone birthday parties until he died in 2015.

Near the middle of the year 2000, I read an article in the *Canadian Jewish News* about a Jewish Museum being built in Berlin, designed by the innovative architect Daniel Libeskind. It would contain archives revealing the contributions Jews made to the development of the arts and sciences as well as to commercial growth in Germany throughout the centuries. As the restitution of our assets was resolved and the archives of our German holdings were of no further use to us, I thought they could be of historical value to the new Jewish Museum Berlin, whose mission is to remember the horrors of the Holocaust and highlight the contributions made to Germany's industrial development by people like my ancestors. They were delighted to receive all that I could send them.

I packed a two-by-four-foot crate with paintings of my grandparents, photographs and balance sheets from the glove factory, and a beautiful bound leather folio the employees had ordered for the celebration of Gebrüder Beckers' fiftieth anniversary celebration, which my father and uncle, the owners, did not attend. I also sent letters and pictures of our time in Germany, including a photograph of my father as a WW I soldier fighting for the Fatherland, and more.

To my surprise, they really enjoyed receiving a little book into which my mother had recorded all the theater performances, operas, and concerts she attended and what she thought of each performance. She began this practice when she was sixteen years old in 1917, and continued until 1985, at which time she wrote into that little book, "And now I happily watch television programs."

I shall now make a confession.

While Ernie was still alive, I often jokingly suggested to him that we should both have facelifts to correct the folds appearing in our necks. Yes, I am a vain woman and did not like what I saw happening to my face, but I was scared to do anything about it until I had my annual checkup with my doctor's female physician's assistant and jokingly shared my concern. She jumped at the chance to recommend an amazingly cautious, careful, capable plastic surgeon she had worked for, sure that I would be pleased with his work.

Accompanied by my new bridge friend, the much younger, sophisticated Candace Dauphinot, whom I learned to love and respect, I went to this fine doctor in Monterey. We both agreed that he had the right approach to not only restore me to a younger look, but also to gently work on my face so that I would age more gracefully and not cringe every time I looked in the mirror. I made an appointment to go under the knife toward the end of 2000 and was instructed to be at Salinas Hospital, thirty miles south of Santa

Candace Dauphinot & Liesel

Cruz, at 7:30 am. As soon as I arrived, I received an injection to relax me, then was visited by an anesthesiologist who, dressed like a character from outer space, explained (while I was in my stupor) that it could be dangerous for a woman of seventy-five to be under anesthesia for more than three hours and that my doctor's operations usually lasted close to six hours.

It would have been much better if I had been given this news before I had donned the hospital gown, but I was ready to have the procedure done and believed that I was healthy enough to tolerate anesthesia for those six hours.

The operation lasted not six, but seven hours. I was told that my physician took more than two-and-a-half hours just to put marks on the spots he intended to cut, in order not to create a distortion that would change my facial expressions. When I awoke wearing an oxygen mask, Candace, who was there to take me home, decided that I needed to stay in the hospital overnight. Obviously I survived; but beyond that, the decision to have this procedure has helped me age more gracefully. I have enjoyed its positive effects for the last twenty-one years.

Lotte Becker on her 100th birthday with granddaughter Lynn Sabloff

Chapter Sixteen
Mother's 100th Birthday and a Return to Chemnitz

MY BROTHER FRED believed that our mother's 100th birthday on January 31, 2001 deserved to be celebrated in the most beautiful surroundings with a gourmet meal, and he made sure that my mother received a certificate of congratulations from the President of the United States. He accomplished these goals with my help, and everyone who attended appreciated his efforts. Our now tiny, barely five-foot-tall mother loved the evening and worked her way up to the podium with her walker to welcome her guests.

My children, Lotte's aged sister-in-law Hertha, and the wonderful couple who so lovingly cared for her for years were all present, as were a distant cousin, Ursula Feist, a younger contemporary who was, like my mother, born in Leipzig, and Cousin Carlos, who flew to Florida all the way from Brazil. He was not going to miss this celebration. But where were all her friends? She had outlived all of them. Ernie and I had friends wintering in Florida, so they joined the festivities, as did Mother's lawyer and accountant, and our investment advisor, Morgan, who came from California.

Lotte Becker was always at her best when surrounded by a group of people. Although her constitution was very frail and macular degeneration did not let her enjoy television (as she had stated in that little book we sent to the Jewish Museum Berlin), her mind was still functioning on all levels, which allowed her to interact graciously with all her guests. The day we were all to return home, we went to her apartment to say goodbye and she accompanied us slowly with her walker down the long corridor. We burst into the marching song "It's a Long Way to Tipperary" to see if this once-athletic woman would pick up her pace, and sure enough, she did. Only three months after the festivities, however, we were notified that she had taken a bad fall which forced her stay in bed, and that a recovery was unlikely.

Hospice was in attendance by the time Fred and I came back to Florida. Our mother was already in a comatose state and passed away very shortly after our visit. She was a feisty, attractive, sportive, community-minded woman who had lived her life fully. She had a husband who adored her, a son who loved her deeply, and I, her daughter, admired her outgoing qualities and tenaciousness. She gave me the opportunity to gain experience and participate in sports, music and dance, and saw to it that I learned to speak English as quickly as possible when we arrived in Canada. But she never gave me her love. I, in turn, was content to simply honor this stylish lady, as one Biblical commandment dictates. In her will, my nontraditional Jewish mother wrote that she wanted to be cremated and have her ashes spread in the Atlantic. As the law demanded this could only take place three miles from shore, Fred and I relinquished this mission to Bill and Jeannie, her caregivers, who owned a boat. They performed the task lovingly when the weather permitted them to venture that far out in the ocean.

Earlier in January, Fred had informed me that he, like former Jewish residents of Chemnitz, had been invited to return to our hometown in the middle of March to participate in their now-annual celebration of a Jewish cultural week. He said that he was not going and suggested I go instead. How much traveling can one do within three months? I was already booked to go to Ireland in late March, which promised to include exceptionally interesting experiences. But another former Chemnitz playmate and twice-removed cousin, Erwin Frank, who had attended this event the previous year, encouraged me to go. He was impressed by the city's mayor, Peter Siefert, who had been elected to that post in 1999 and felt it his duty to attempt to rectify the grave mistakes of the past. He encouraged our hometown citizens to become engaged in Jewish culture and to help build a synagogue for the approximately three hundred Russian Jews who had settled in Chemnitz—the first synagogue since the old one was destroyed by the Nazis in 1938.

So off I went to partake in the festivities, joining nine former Chemnitzers returning from the countries to which they had escaped in the 1930s. We became a cohesive group in a no time, and I particularly enjoyed the company of the two Engelberg brothers and their wives, one of whom we discovered was related by marriage to another distant cousin of mine in Britain. Simon Beck came from Switzerland; he and I have been particularly good friends since we met in Germany and have corresponded regularly over the last twenty years. It was he who recently sent me a detailed schedule of our week in Chemnitz, the structure of which was vague in my memory.

Jewish Cultural Week in Chemnitz. L: Engelbergs & Liesel; far R: Simon Beck

Initially, I was only able to recall what to me were two surreal experiences. The first was a gathering of 300–400 Germans at the local museum to open an exhibit of paintings by a Russian Jewish artist, with the mayor of Chemnitz in attendance and klezmer music playing in the background. We nine were the guests of honor. The mayor welcomed us and made a sincere, valiant attempt to apologize in the name of all present for the terrible wrongs done to Germany's Jews during the Nazi era. During another evening, in the company of enthusiastic Germans, we were treated to dinner in a restaurant named Shalom, again with a wonderful klezmer band.

I just could not believe that all these typically German men and women in attendance were entirely regretful of their past and now admired our traditions. That has been and will remain a question for me my entire life—because no matter where or in what decades I have lived, anti-Semitism continues. On the other hand, when asked by a radio reporter (who held a microphone in front of me on our bus tour of the city) what my feelings were towards the offspring of those who had participated in the torture and murder of Jews, I responded without hesitation that I will never forget or forgive what happened but that I do not hold the children responsible for their fathers' sins.

During our stay in Chemnitz, we were again impressed with how highly active our forebears had been in making this the textile center of Germany, comparable to Manchester in England. WW II had decimated that entire industry and 40 percent of the city. The enormous sculpture of the head of Karl Marx in the main square was evidence that in 1948, the city became an East German Soviet satellite city, changed its name to Karl-Marx-Stadt, and was at that time rebuilt with the typically drab *Krushchyovkas* apartments described in my trip to Russia. By 2001, these buildings had been refurbished and painted bright, cheerful colors, the name Chemnitz was restored, and the city was in the throes of trying to reestablish industrial growth. But why did the Karl Marx sculpture still dominate the central square?

On a bright sunny day, Siegmund Rotstein, the Jewish community leader I had met in 1992 when I first visited Chemnitz, led us to the site where a very modern synagogue was under construction with the assistance of city finances. He explained that the substantial number of Russian Jews who had left the Soviet Union to settle in Germany warranted building synagogues in Dresden, Leipzig, and Chemnitz, and that we would meet a group of the local members of this new congregation at a Sabbath service and dinner that evening.

Our next stop was the Jewish cemetery, which was covered in a light blanket of snow. Mr. Rotstein had been instrumental in its restoration. We were all impressed to find it in such pristine condition. I walked to the marble headstones of the Becker family graves and was so glad to see them restored to perfection.

While at the cemetery, our group leader introduced me to a most remarkable Christian gentleman, Jürgen Nitsche, who was compiling the history of the 3,500 Jews who had lived and worked in Chemnitz. He felt strongly about the importance of gathering all their stories and wanted to place these beside a picture of each family's grave in a 500-page coffee table book entitled *The Jews of Chemnitz.*

Rotstein, Liesel, Nitsche

Jürgen became a friend. He already knew a great deal of my family history. I promised to write a brief story to be placed beside the picture of the Becker graves in his book, which not only documented the history of all the Jews in the cemetery but

also included a list of articles about religious practices, education, charities, Jews in the military, business (there are pictures of my uncle and my father, their factory workrooms and the interior of my uncle's house) and other professions, as well as patrons and collectors of the arts, and the reemerging Jewish congre-

"Juden in Chemnitz" gation in 1945. I sent Dr. Nitsche a picture of eight community members—my Uncle Carl and Aunt Erna among them—at a planning meeting for the construction of a Jewish golf course in 1932, which he used for the cover of the book that has now graced my coffee table for the last fifteen years.

While at the cemetery, Jürgen gave me exciting news. The aged widow of one of my father's trusted German lawyers, Mr. Willy

Schumann, was still alive and hoped that I would pay her a visit. She had something she wanted to show me. I agreed without hesitation and he took me to visit Ms. Schumann that very afternoon. You may remember that our family left Germany after Arthur Weiner, one of Gebrüder Becker's lawyers, was brutally murdered in April 1933. Willy Schumann, Arthur Weiner's non-Jewish partner, came to Holland several times in the mid-1930s to confer with my dad and Uncle Karl about keeping their German business running smoothly in their absence. Sitting at my computer in 2021 and recalling these visits, my curiosity was aroused. If I googled his name, would I find more information about Willy Schumann?

Two articles popped up and I learned that this good man, in his effort to keep Jewish companies functional, had to straddle the former laws of Germany and the Nazi-imposed restrictions of the era. Adolf Hitler had wasted no time. He was sworn in by President Hindenburg as Chancellor of Germany in March of 1933 and in April the shocking anti-Jewish mandate—German citizens were not to seek advice from Jewish lawyers or visit Jewish doctors, to boycott all Jewish establishments, and not to buy anything in stores owned by Jews—was published in all German newspapers.

Those were the restrictions Willy Schumann had to deal with when my farsighted father and uncle led their families to safety in Holland.

As Jürgen and I entered the Schumanns' home, we were warmly greeted by his daughter and his elderly wife, Uwe.

"Dont Buy from Jews"

Mrs. Schumann expressed her happiness to meet the daughter of Arthur Becker, for whom she and her husband had such high regard. As she talked, she clutched letters in her hand. She told us that my father had enclosed the letters in the food parcels he had sent them during the war. Of course, I could not wait to read them. I was so proud that my thoughtful, loyal father did not turn his back on those Germans he respected and instead supplied them with needed nutritional products and letters of encouragement. I regret that I did not ask if I could have those letters or have copies made, which I would have sent to the Jewish Museum Berlin. It only occurred to me fifteen years later, and when I contacted Jürgen, he informed me that all Schumanns' relatives had left the area. I would never see those letters again.

That evening, we had the pleasure of meeting with approximately forty Russian Jews for a Sabbath service and dinner at the Jewish Community Center. Siegmund Rostein, who led the service, explained that the community could not yet afford to hire a permanent rabbi but that the three cities within 50 km, Chemnitz, Leipzig and Dresden, shared the services of a rabbi and a cantor who came to each city in turn, every three weeks. He also mentioned that several of the Russian immigrants had knowledge of Yiddish from their ancestors but had never learned to read Hebrew nor been exposed to Jewish history. Yet on that day, they participated joyfully in the Sabbath service and sang the prayers from a transliteration. Throughout the meal we conversed with those who had knowledge of German or English, but there was little opportunity to learn more of their backgrounds or what had brought them to this community, which was building a house of prayer to accommodate them.

During our stay, our hometown also gave us the opportunity for two guided tours. We were all interested in going to Dresden, the city that had been known as the German "Florence on the Elbe," the center of European culture. My parents had attended performances at the beautiful baroque Semper Opera House before it was decimated during WW II and my mother recorded the qualities of those performances in her little book, which is now in the Jewish Museum Berlin. In 2001, it was good to see that Dresden was in the throes of rebuilding its former splendor and that a little synagogue had been constructed overlooking the beautiful Elbe River. We also spent a delightful, lighthearted afternoon in the winter wonderland of the Ore Mountain range, at the base of which Chemnitz was built. It was there that I had my first skiing lesson as a six-year-old. The beautiful area is world famous for the Erzgebirge wood-carved Christmas ornaments that are a pleasure to behold.

Chemnitz is only 30 km from Leipzig, my mother's hometown where, as a twelve-year-old in 1937, I had spent a week visiting my Omi and Opa, Grete and Josef Frank. I was curious to revisit the "German Capital of Music," which celebrates the music of J.S. Bach, Felix Mendelssohn, and Richard Wagner. Through our restitution lawyer, I contacted one of his assistants, a young Chemnitzer named Gert Hornfleck, who kindly offered to drive me to Leipzig for the day. Simon Beck, my new acquaintance, was happy to join us on this excursion. Gert drove us past my grandparents' former residence. In moments of reflection, I recalled how I loved running and playing in the beautiful park a few steps from their home. We then visited the St. Thomas Church, built in 1202, where Bach was the music director and composed the great body of his works between 1723 until his death in 1750, and where Wagner and Mendelssohn, my favorite composer, director and conductor, performed their compositions. After a tour of the city, Simon and I urged Gert to take us to a typical German restaurant where we could enjoy the familiar tastes of goulash with red cabbage and knoedel. It was interesting to spend time with a young man who had grown up in East Germany under the rule of Soviet Russia. Gert told us he had received excellent schooling and been exposed to wonderful sports programs, but that the Communists took no initiative to bring industries back to East Germany. He and his cohorts were disappointed to be left so far behind the achievements of the West. This inequity was noticeable at the time of our visit in 2001 and is still evident to a lesser degree as of this writing in 2021.

Jewish Cultural Week ended the next day at a luncheon in the *Rathaus* or city hall, with the charming, innovative mayor and members of the city's legislature. We nine "Honored Citizens" were asked to sign "The Golden Book of Chemnitz." As I put pen to paper, I realized that I was given this honor in memory of all my family members who had contributed to making Chemnitz the vibrant city it once was. It was a memorable week on many levels, and as we went our separate ways, I believe each of us had different reactions to what we had just experienced. I am not clear if we were meant to be the only beneficiaries of this annual event or whether it was also to help promote Chemnitz and its citizens as an East German city that remembered its troubled past and continued to make amends, just as Berlin, Hamburg, Munich, and others have done since the 1960s.

Sadly, no place in this beautiful world escapes the discord humans create for religious, ethnic, economic, political, or even purely personal reasons. I had just been part of a city's attempt to overcome those discords. How could I forego a visit to Ireland, when the Elderhostel travel company had permission for travelers to witness the beginning of the end of the painful struggles between the Catholics (led by the IRA) and the Protestants in Northern Ireland (led by the Orange Order)? I went on that trip with Marion Steinmetz, another friend I had met at the Santa Cruz Bridge Club, despite that fact that it was my fourth journey in four months.

Just as when Ernie and I took a trip to Israel where we were students at three universities, that is what we became when we arrived in Dublin. We came prepared by having read the recommended books, and during our three days in Dublin, we sat at our desks every morning to listen to local personalities deliver interesting lectures. However, I was chomping at the bit to see the sites, so Marion joined me in skipping class one morning to visit the local synagogue. As we approached, we saw that it was under lock and key with fences guarding its portals, like the synagogues I had tried to visit in Florence, Marseille, and Turkey. Could a city that had two Jewish mayors for the last seven decades also be plagued by anti-Semitism? After that, I followed the rules. I particularly enjoyed the world-renowned University of Dublin and the evening Literary Pub Crawl, led by actors reciting poetry and telling stories of Ireland's famous authors as we walked from pub to pub with the goal of downing a pint at each stop.

As we motored toward Galway, our next destination, I hoped to see fields the color of the Irish shamrock, the green for which Ireland is so famous. But we only saw acres of gray bog which, when dried, would become the squares of peat that are a much-needed fuel for most Irish households. I had signed up for a three-night homestay with a family in Galway that used such fuel to heat their house. Since I did not keep a diary and cannot recall my hosts' names, I will call them Liam and Shannon. Liam, my nice-looking, well-dressed host, awaited me in a parking lot. I do not remember how the conversation turned to bridge before I stepped into his car, but when he found out that both Marion and I played, he insisted we play at his bridge club that evening. My hostess Shannon was a tall, attractive woman who welcomed me into her humble home and introduced me to the older of their three teenaged children, who seemed well-educated, well read, and completely at ease in their conversation with adults.

Marion and I were both astonished how comfortable and engaging were all the young Irish people with whom we exchanged ideas. There was no hemming or hawing, no, "You know, you know…" Unfortunately, my hosts' youngest boy needed special care, and Shannon also revealed that her husband was unemployed though Ireland's economy was booming at that time.

That first evening in Galway, Liam picked Marion up at her homestay and we were off to the local bridge club, where my friend and I were partners and drinking hard liquor became part of the game. At the start of the game, Liam placed a tall gin and tonic on my table, and of course I had to reciprocate. Then another one was placed in front of me. It was a jolly, unforgettable evening but I was uncomfortable having this unemployed man spend money on my drinks. When we returned to their home, one block of peat was hardly enough to heat their house, but a second may not have been affordable. Or perhaps they were all hardy and had adapted to cooler temperatures. I was assigned the youngest child's metal bed, which stood in an alcove with a cooled hot water bottle awaiting me.

Although it was not the lap of luxury, I thoroughly enjoyed the experience of sharing time with the bright, devoted Shannon, who introduced me to her charming extended family. She also shared her marital problems, and that she would have loved to go to work but was needed at home. The money Elderhostel paid for hosting was the one way she could augment their income. As for Liam, I did not see him after our slightly inebriated evening of bridge. I left that family hoping they, like the country to their north, would find a way to resolve their troubles.

From the charming fishing town of Galway, we motored through fertile fields towards Belfast in Northern Ireland. After sixty years of conflict during which thousands were killed, the Catholic members of the IRA and their Protestant opponents, a group called the Orange Order, had crafted the tenuous Good Friday Agreement with the amazing former US Secretary of State George Mitchell as mediator. The 1998 agreement was an historic compromise. For the first time, the two governments, along with parties from across the divide, agreed on a new political framework for Northern Ireland and committed themselves to working together to sustain the peace. We were the first Elderhostel group to meet with representatives of both sides of the new government and to attend a session of Parliament. We were also shown vivid memorial paintings of past battles on the walls of homes inhabited by members of the IRA.

An attractive young Catholic receptionist at our hotel was willing to share her perception of the accord. She had been part of a group of young people from both sides who attended a weekend retreat with the aim to get to know each other and learn to accept each other's differences. She said it was a wonderful experience, but she was sad that those good feelings dissipated when the Orangemen continued their annual march through her neighborhood.

Despite setbacks, the people in Northern Ireland have persisted and are making the agreement work. I believe the world should look at this as an example of how to resolve all kinds of personal, political, economic, or religious conflicts with the help of well-trained, caring, accredited mediators.

I returned home that spring, and throughout the summer enjoyed my favorite games of golf and duplicate bridge, Sabbath dinners, and discussions with good friends. As captain of the Ladies' Golf Club in Santa Cruz, I also tried to apply whatever conflict resolution skills I might possess to the problems that arose there.

Having received an invitation to attend the opening of the Jewish Museum Berlin, I boarded another plane September 8, 2001,

for the three-day celebration. My friend Judy Haber, who had plans for further excursions in Europe, joined me in Berlin. Architect Daniel Libeskind had designed the museum to represent a broken Mogen David, the six-cornered Star of David. It also incorporated a large smokestack reminiscent of those at Auschwitz. I found the

Jewish Museum Berlin architecture; Mogen David

slanted walls of the interior disturbing, but that might have been just what the architect wanted people to feel.

And I was disappointed in the exhibit. The original reason for creating this museum had been to remember the contributions made by Jews to the development of Germany throughout the ages. That idea seemed to have been forgotten. Historic items donated by people like me were displayed in random fashion in narrow, winding display corridors. Happily, Judy and I did discover one contribution of ours in a small glass case near the entrance—my brother's and my German passports with their swastikas. I have since received brochures of exhibits from this highly regarded museum and have been unimpressed with any of them. However, I recently accessed their website and was excited to see remarkably beautiful, dramatic changes made under a new director in 2018. It is too bad my travel days are now behind me.

On September 11, the final day of the festivities, I returned to our hotel room right behind Judy, who was staring in horror at a picture of a plane that had hit the first Twin Tower in New York. While we listened to the announcer describing the event, we watched another plane attack the second tower and saw those majestic buildings crumble. Was this the beginning of a war? All airline travel came to a halt, including my flight home. We were not in Santa Cruz during the earthquake in 1989 nor when a fire burned part of our house, and now again I was far from home when this tragedy occurred.

A total of 2997 people died in New York, at the Pentagon, and in a field in Pennsylvania where passengers tried to stop the four terrorists who took over the cockpit on United Airlines Flight 93 destined for the White House, the Capitol Building or Camp David. This shocked the entire world and altered Americans' view of Muslims dramatically. I now had to add Islamophobia to my vocabulary.

Nancy Sabloff in her ceramics studio, Hawaii

Chapter Seventeen
Auschwitz, Budapest and Other Travels

BY THE BEGINNING OF 2002, I was well into the fourth quarter of my life, residing in Santa Cruz (which has the best climate in our universe) and living among good friends and a considerable number of acquaintances. I had nothing to complain about.

I had long ago come to terms with the fact that it was unlikely any of my three children would marry or that I would become a grandmother. The joy of holding the next generation in my arms or seeing my children as parents was not in the cards.

However, I was content that all three had settled in places they liked living. Lynn moved to the Dominican Republic to administer a small hotel owned by Montreal friends. She settled in Cabrera, near other expatriates from Quebec and the US, and built an attractive house on a remote hill. Nancy finally made her home in Hawaii, which suited this former singer, paralegal, and massage therapist. An accomplished craftsperson, she now produces beautiful ceramics. She, too, owns her home and studio and will never go hungry, as avocados fall on her roof, bananas and tangelos overflow her kitchen, and she recently found ginger growing on her property. My bright, handsome son Daniel made Vancouver his home after graduating from the University of British Columbia and had yet to find his métier. He still checks on his mother at 8:30 every morning. I had only visited my daughters three times each because I do not function on all cylinders in hot, damp environments. Fortunately, Nancy and Daniel can come to visit regularly.

In 2002, we celebrated Fred's 80th birthday in Toronto. After a few more healthy years, my kind brother's memory began to deteriorate, and eventually he needed help around the clock. We spoke often, and during the times I returned to be with friends in Montreal (where I had the intense pleasure of staying with my pie-making teacher Ruth Cohen), I would return home via Toronto to spend time with Fred. In Toronto, Ernie's cousin Eric and his wife Ruthie, whom I grew to love and admire, invited me to stay with them. Those visits also gave me the opportunity to enjoy catching up with the children of former Montreal neighbors and friends who had moved to Toronto because of the Quiet Revolution.

All of this meant that nobody was dependent on me or needed me to be around at any specific time. I was a free agent, with the good fortune to have adequate funds to satisfy my desire to travel extensively, partake in competitive golf and bridge (because competition makes me want to continue to improve), read, go to museums, and experiment in my kitchen with never-tried recipes when friends came to dinner.

On my trip to Japan with the Overseas Adventure Travel company that I loved, one of our companions stated that he had been to sixty countries. This started everybody present recalling the number they had visited. To my surprise, I could recall setting foot in fifty countries, including Bermuda, Cuba, and other smaller nations. There are so many wonderful, broadening things I experienced on each of my journeys to China and Tibet, India, Thailand and Cambodia, the former Yugoslavia, Bosnia and Herzegovina, Slovenia, Turkey, and other countries; but that is not what this story is meant to be about. I do, however, want to take you with me on two more trips relating to our departure from Germany—one of which will take us back to Israel and another to Eastern Europe, where I visited Auschwitz.

In the winter of 2004, Miriam and Noel Fishman urged me to join them in Israel for the bar mitzvah of their second grandson, Tsachi. I was always ready to hop on another plane. Not only did I want to participate in this event, but the trip also gave me an opportunity to revisit the friends Ernie and I had made when we were Volunteers for Israel. The Fishman's daughter Brenda and husband Steve had "made *aliyah*," the term for Jews who emigrate to Israel, which means "to ascend or go towards God in the Promised Land." They now lived in Beit Shemesh, which translates to "House of the Sun." This community of English-speaking modern Orthodox Jews, 30 km west of Jerusalem at the bottom of a hill, seemed a village of like-minded people who all knew each other.

When a Jewish thirteen-year-old celebrates his or her bar or bat mitzvah, he or she makes their "first *aliyah*" when they are called up to the *bimah*—the raised platform from which prayers are read or chanted—to recite a part of that week's portion of the Torah in Hebrew. In addition, they also recite a portion from the Prophets, or *haftorah*, and can read an original prayer or explain the meaning of the *haftorah* portion they just read. The youngsters study under the tutelage of a rabbi or a cantor for months to be capable and comfortable in performing these rituals.

Tsachi performed like a pro and made his entire family so proud. He is now in his thirties and continues to be admired for all he has achieved since that day. As the bar mitzvah activities ended, I strolled around Kibbutz Tzora, which operated a state-of-the-art dairy near my hotel. As I toured the well-equipped kibbutz, I recalled my own experience with milking cows, and was fascinated as well as appalled to learn these cows never go out to pasture but are on a special diet in their stalls to produce twice as much milk as the cows I looked after. The milk is even tested for bacteria while the milking machines are still on their udders. I did not like this picture. Cows should be able to wander and feed in picturesque green pastures. But how much pasture does this tiny country, which is still trying to make its desert bloom, have? Had I been able to release the cows and herd them a mile to the south, they would have trampled all over the important archeological excavation of Tell es-Safi, a Philistine town where it is believed Goliath once resided.

Happily, Brenda, Tsachi's mom, found time to drive me around Beit Shemesh. At that time, more than 2,000 Black Ethiopian

Jewish refugees still lived in their midst in what had once been a development town created to help these immigrants to adapt to Israeli life, a process that was not yet complete. We then drove up a steep hill we had seen from her home, and Brenda explained that the higher we climbed, the more orthodox the communities became and that she, a modern Orthodox, would not be welcome among the Haredi, or ultra-orthodox Jews who lived on the summit. At the time of my visit, Beit Shemesh had 65,900 inhabitants. By 2019, that number swelled to 124,371, of which 73 percent are Orthodox. The city was governed by a highly regarded Orthodox female mayor who was a very competent mediator, critical to a city made up of so many different Jewish sects.

On another day, I took the comfortable wide-body diesel train to Tel Aviv to meet with Lore Frank, another twice-removed cousin from Chemnitz with whom I had plans to view a collection of Archipenko sculptures that had been donated to that city's museum by the family Goeritz, who were familiar to us and had been amongst the most renowned art collectors in Chemnitz. When Tel Aviv came into view, I was stunned by the enormous number of skyscrapers that had grown since my last visit in 1992.

As it is my habit to be on time or even ten minutes early for an appointment, I wandered around the gallery while waiting for Lore. It is impossible to describe the emotions that overcame me when I found myself standing in front of my favorite painting by Max Liebermann that had hung in our dining room in Germany,

Hammock (Siesta), Slevogt

Holland, and Canada. When I recovered my equilibrium and walked on, incredible as it seemed, two more of our paintings were displayed: another by Liebermann, and one by the artist Max Slevogt, of two men relaxing in hammocks. It was my father's favorite because it inspired him to relax. As I read the captions beside these paintings, I learned they were on loan to the museum. The name of the owner was not mentioned, but I had my suspicions of who the owner might be.

My parents had sold these and five other paintings, lovingly chosen during the early years of their marriage, to a gallery in Munich in the 1970s, when Dad retired and they moved to Florida. Fred and I were each given the opportunity to choose two paintings from their collection of twelve before the sale. I still love the ones I chose, which hang in my California living room. I remember that the owners of the gallery told my father that a Jewish family, who had emigrated to Israel during the war and lived part time there and part time in Munich, had purchased the paintings. I believed they had loaned them to the Tel Aviv Museum for others to appreciate. I wanted to photograph the paintings in this environment but was not granted permission, even after having told those in charge their history.

When Lore arrived, though she was a distant relative I had never met, we were completely at ease with one another, just as I am with most people who share my history. We promptly searched for the donation made by the Goeritz family and found it in a small alcove where ten or so small, beautifully executed, fully formed Archipenko sculptures were displayed on a cement slab. To me, these exquisitely carved sculptures looked like maquettes from which foundries would make larger versions, just as the sculptor Harry Marinsky—whom Ernie and I had met on a trip to Italy—had his small sculptures enlarged at the Pietrasanta foundry near Carrara in that country.

After that exciting afternoon, I packed my bag and got back on the comfortable diesel train to spend a few days with Barbara Hirscheimer in Haifa. From there I ventured once more to Kfar Tavor for a wonderful three-day visit with my former Volunteers for Israel hosts, the Dvirs, then met Etie Golan from Ma'ale Adumim in Jerusalem before concluding my last trip to Israel. My memento of that journey is a menorah made of nine individual beautifully shaped brass candlesticks, an eightieth birthday present to myself that I could not leave behind, which I now light annually on Chanukah.

My eightieth birthday celebration was at the Steins' house. Mimi and Candace Dauphinot outdid themselves gathering friends for a special evening, with fabulous food and speeches that I will always remember. Ruth and Bernie Issenman's daughter Tina and another friend had collected photos of the various stages of my life to produce an album. Each photo was artistically decorated with the flags, crests, and symbols of the countries in which they were taken. It made me feel like such a lucky person!

I am not certain which year it was, in the second part of the first decade of 2000, when I booked a two-and-a-half-week tour to eastern Europe to see historic sites of Warsaw and the beauty of Prague, and to explore the interesting cities of Buda and Pest. Going to Auschwitz, although important to this story, was part of the tour but not my reason for taking this trip. Throughout my entire adult life, I believed it to be incumbent upon me to watch all documentaries about the Holocaust, read the stories by survivors like Elie Wiesel and Viktor Frankl, go to Dachau, and visit Holocaust museums so I can pass this part of history on to others. I was so familiar with what happened at Auschwitz that I believed that walking the grounds and seeing the gas ovens and dilapidated barracks where my fellow Jews and other "chosen" people tried to sleep three deep on wooden planks while listening to the nightmares of others, would not enlighten me further and might be very disturbing.

But it turned out to be one of the most important parts of this story, because I took the letter cousin Kurt, the Ritchie Boy, had sent me from the Jewish Museum in Prague, documenting my grandmother's train ride to Auschwitz. I put the letter—along with the six, twenty-five-word Red Cross letters she wrote before she was arrested in Amsterdam, and a picture of that fine-looking lady— into a folder that I hoped to pass around to other passengers on our bus ride to the concentration camp, if the tour leader agreed.

The day I was to leave California, Anita and Dick Arthur, friends from bridge club, picked me up at six in the morning. Dick questioned whether I had all my documents and I responded in the affirmative. But I was wrong. After they deposited me at the airport,

I realized my passport was not with me—I had left it in my copy machine. I returned home and was incredibly lucky to be able to fly to Poland the next day, or I might have missed going to the camp. The leader of the tour greeted me the night I arrived. I told her that I had a grandmother who had been killed at Auschwitz, and what I had prepared. She thought it was an excellent idea to tell my grandmother's story while the folder was passed around on the bus as we motored to Auschwitz.

I returned to my room, content that I had arrived in good time to join the thirty-four other passengers on this journey. I love submerging myself in a deep bathtub and took the opportunity to jump into the very deep, narrow one in this old hotel. But I found myself in trouble; I could not get out of this wonderful tub. There was no bell to ring for help and no bar to pull me up, and it was too narrow for me to turn around to get on my knees. Coming to terms with this ridiculous situation, I lay back ready to relax for the night in a tub, when I saw a pipe that I might be able to reach. I had to work hard to grab it and pull myself up.

Clean and rested, I met the fellow travelers with whom I was to explore the city of Warsaw, reconstructed from having been 85 percent destroyed by the Nazis during WW II. According to Polish writer Leopold Tyrmand, "One of the philosophers calculated that Varsovians inhaled four bricks of dust each year at that time."

Despite that, they rebuilt their city in its former image, using stones the destruction left behind and paintings by Bernardo Belletto (1720–1780) as the plan to achieve this. They did not, however, rebuild the Warsaw Ghetto, but created a dramatic memorial of the stones that remained at that site.

Belletto painting used to rebuild Warsaw

On the following day, we drove 327 km to Auschwitz and, as planned, my folder was passed around as we neared the camp. I was given the mic

Discovering Their Fates
My Visit to Auschwitz

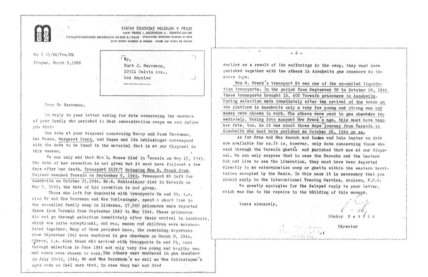

Letter from Jewish Museum Prague to Kurt Herrmann regarding the fate of his parents, Harry & Rosa Herrmann, and Liesel's grandmother, Margaret (Grete) Frank

From page 1: "...Margaret Frank....Transport XXIV/7 bringing Mrs. M. Frank from Holland reached Terezín on September 6, 1944."

From page 2: "...Mrs. M. Frank's transport Et was one of the so-called liquidation transports. In the period from September 28 to October 28, 1944 these transports brought 18,402 Terezín prisoners to Auschwitz. During selection made immediately after the arrival of the train on the platform in Auschwitz, only a very few young and strong men and women were chosen to work. The others were sent to gas chambers immediately. Taking into account Mrs. Frank's age, this must have been her fate, too. As it was about three days' journey from Terezín to Auschwitz, she must have perished on October 26, 1944 or so."

Above: Margaret (Grete) Frank

Translation, Red Cross letter:
"14 April, 1943. Am healthy in spite of the very worst times. Anne takes good care of me. Best regards to Beckers, Rudi & relatives. Hope you are all well. With love, your grateful Grete"

Liesel finds grandmother Margaret Frank's suitcase (left center), Auschwitz

to tell the group my grandmother's story. You may remember that my maternal grandparents would not leave Leipzig for Holland until 1938; my grandfather died early in 1940 and my grandmother was fearful of crossing an already dangerous ocean to join us in Canada. When the Germans invaded Holland, she, like all Jews, was in danger. Because Canada was an enemy country, she could not write to us and was only permitted to send twenty-five-word Red Cross letters to her brother, who had fled with his family to Cali, Colombia.

In four of those six letters that are in my possession, she wrote that she was well taken care of and thinking of all her loved ones, but in the last two you sensed that conditions were deteriorating, that she knew what was about happen to her though she could not express those thoughts on paper. I translated those letters written in German for my fellow travelers, of whom only two were Jewish. There was no way to judge the effect of my brief talk and the contents of the folder, but I was satisfied that they would enter Auschwitz knowing a personal story of one individual who succumbed to the gas chambers that we would see.

As we walked through a gate like the one in Dachau announcing *Arbeit Macht Frei,* I stayed with the tour but left it when we were shown a mockup of how this horrible camp was planned. How could humans make such an intricate architectural plan to kill millions of other people? Miserable as I was, I wandered the halls with displays of reading glasses, artificial limbs, hair, shoes, suitcases and more that had been possessions of those the Nazis tortured or murdered. I found myself standing in front of the victims' suitcases when one of my fellow travelers came and told me that she thought my grandmother's suitcase was there. She led me to a window through which I could see a small suitcase with "Margaret Frank, Holland" and her date of birth written on it. After getting over the shock, I asked a fellow traveler to please take a picture with my camera— not only of the suitcase, but of me looking at it.

That picture turned out to be special because as I look from outside the display, my image is also reflected inside. It emphasizes that, if not for my amazingly good fortune, I could have suffered the same fate as my grandmother.

The Jewish couple offered to say Kaddish with me, the Hebrew memorial prayer that Jews recite when they lose a loved one. After we said "Amen," I was content that my grandmother had finally been memorialized after so many years. I was glad to have brought that folder and given my talk. It all led to the recognition of her suitcase, which otherwise I might have missed. The folder with those few documents has stayed intact and I have added a few more relevant documents. That entire package accompanies me whenever I am invited to talk about my background.

All that I saw and did on the rest of that trip faded into the background after that unbelievably emotional experience. I have no intention of writing a travelogue, yet cannot help but mention how I enjoyed spending a couple of days in the charming city of Kraków. It surrounds a large hill on which stand the Wawel Royal Castle and the Wawel Cathedral, with buildings that trace back to 940 AD. This World Heritage Site is where Polish monarchs were crowned and buried. In the center of the city, where likable Pope John Paul II used to live and 63,000 Jews had made their homes throughout centuries, is a beautiful square with a highly decorated church. Four times every hour, a trumpeter blows his instrument from the highest tower in the direction of the former city gates, a tradition that goes back to the fourteenth century to keep the gatekeepers alert to potential invaders. The 1:00 pm rendition of this hourly event is now broadcast throughout all Poland.

Around the corner from the square, I came across a small museum

Lady with the Ermine

where, to my great surprise and delight, I saw the gorgeous, well-known painting *Lady with the Ermine* by Leonard da Vinci hanging in an unknown gallery. When I researched the history of the painting, I found that it had been painted with the ermine not because she loved that animal, but because she had been the lover of Da Vinci's patron, a duke whose nickname translated to "ermine." If I had to choose between the *Mona Lisa* and that painting, I would choose the latter without a moment's hesitation. Before our departure from Kraków, we also visited the ghetto built by the Nazis in 1941 for the 15,000 workers they needed. The rest of the city's 48,000 Jews who lived there were deported and then annihilated.

When we arrived in the beautiful city of Prague it was overrun with tourists, which made it difficult to appreciate the historic buildings on Castle Square and even harder to cross the famous bridges without being bumped about. However, there was one quiet place to visit—the small and third-oldest Jewish cemetery in Europe, in the old Ghetto of Prague where 200,000 Jews were buried, twelve deep, between 1439 and 1787. "Each crooked tombstone tells a story, crying out its eerie song of pogroms, fires, and floods," penned one writer. On headstones written in Hebrew or Czech were 8,000 features or writings that symbolized family names or professions. For example, a bunch of grapes denoted fertility and wisdom, a quill for a writer, scissors for a tailor, and books on a shelf to describe a rabbi. I would have learned a great deal more about those who were buried there if I had hired a guide to translate the Czech or Hebrew writings.

The Prague Jewish Museum, which had issued the letter describing my grandmother's trip to Auschwitz, was just around the corner from the cemetery. I am certain they would have had records of the 669 children that British-born Nicholas Winton, a successful London banker and humanitarian, rescued in 1938 as part of the *Kindertransport* that brought 10,000 European Jewish children to England, where compassionate Jews and Gentiles welcomed them into their homes. One of those 10,000 was my cousin Edith Twelkemeyer from Nordhausen, Germany. A Scottish Protestant family gave her shelter and adopted her when they learned of her parents' death, and grateful Edith converted to their faith.

The CBS program *60 Minutes* reviewed the 1988 BBC broadcast *That's Life!* which revealed the now-grown children and their offspring to their rescuer, Nicholas Winton, and his wife. By that time, their numbers had grown to more than 6,000, many of whom gathered to pay homage to this courageous man who had saved them but never taken credit for his virtuous deeds. Like Captain Gustav Schroeder of the German transatlantic luxury liner the *St. Louis*, Winton is memorialized in the Holocaust Memorial in Jerusalem. The world would be a much better place if everyone took Nicholas Winton's motto to heart: "That goodness properly understood is not passive but that the world requires individuals who not only refrain from harming others but energetically seek out those in need of help."

Before motoring to Budapest and delving into more Holocaust history, we made a small detour to Karlsbad (now Karlovy Vary). As it is only 63 km from Chemnitz, my parents often vacationed there to be rejuvenated by the water of the city's hot springs. We were not going there to take the cure, but to visit the Moser Glass Museum and store. My kitchen cupboard contains the remnants of art deco Moser glasses my parents had bought there, with their damaged edges ground down, so I was excited to enter this facility. I loved the whole collection but fell in love with six beveled amber shot glasses that were perfect for holding the kosher Manischewitz

wine we bless on the Sabbath. No, I did not need them, nor anything else for that matter, but I could not resist them. They are now in the cupboard with the other inherited Moser glasses. My guests love to sip their wine from these little beauties.

Most cities are built on the shores of large rivers. Budapest came into view, the old city of Buda on the west side of the Danube— with its castle and the impressive Matthias Church where I heard a wonderful concert—and Pest, with large parliament buildings decorating the eastern shore. At the time of our visit, authoritarian leaders occupied those impressive government buildings. The two cities are united by a series of bridges, of which the Széchenyi Chain Bridge is a beautiful example. The economy was in bad shape and anti-Semitism was on the rise again in Hungary, despite memorials that should have reminded the population that more than 400,000 Hungarian Jews were deported in 1944, and the 200,000 who remained in Budapest would also have been deported were it not for Swedish architect, diplomat, and humanitarian Raoul Wallenberg. With the help of other caring persons, Wallenberg issued protective passports to Jews and sheltered them in thirty safe houses that together formed the core of the "international ghetto" in Budapest. He was able to save a substantial number from deportation and to obtain visas for 3,000 who escaped to safe harbors. Sadly, when Soviet forces entered Budapest in 1945, Raoul Wallenberg was detained on suspicion of espionage and imprisoned in the infamous Lubyanka prison in Moscow, where he is said to have died in 1947.

Next to the impressive Dohány Street Synagogue, the largest in all of Europe, is Raoul Wallenberg Holocaust Memorial Park, with an iron image of a weeping willow tree. From its branches hang

"Shoes on the Danube Bank"

iron name tags of Jews imprinted with the numbers that were tattooed on their wrists. Another memorial is comprised of sixty pairs of iron shoes of different shapes and sizes nailed to a cement walkway on the east shore of the Danube, only 980 feet from the Parliament. This memorial, entitled *Shoes on the Danube Bank*, commemorates the 20,000 Jews who were told to remove their shoes (which were in demand) before being brutally shot by members of the Arrow Cross Party and left to drift down the river. While the Arrow Cross Party was in power from 1944–1945, they expelled 80,000 of the 100,000 Jews that Wallenberg had saved before murdering the remaining 20,000.

It is true that the events of WW II have shaped my life to a great degree. They have also made me aware of and concerned for other groups or individuals who suffer similar forms of discrimination. I am fully aware that I have had the good fortune to live in countries which, during my lifetime, have suffered comparatively minor anti-Semitic events compared to those in the 1930s and '40s.

Chapter Eighteen
I Retire My Suitcase

BY THE TIME I entered my mid-eighties, a considerable number of my good friends and acquaintances had passed away. Among them was the vibrant Ruth Issenman, my longtime friend from Montreal who had been influential in our move to Santa Cruz, and with whose family we celebrated so many Friday nights recalling the adventures we shared. Of our *chavurah*, the friendship group which numbered ten in the 1990s, only three, including me, were still alive. My younger, longtime friends—the Krazs, Steins, and Phil and Jenny Welty, my wonderful neighbors—now became my Santa Cruz family. I still played golf and tested my bridge skills at the Santa Cruz Bridge Club. At the club, I continued to meet new people and develop good friends with whom I socialized, shared books, went to the theater, and rode up to San Francisco to see the latest art exhibits at the de Young Museum and the Legion of Honor.

Before retiring my large suitcase, I had one last trip on my bucket list. In 2013 I traveled to Sicily with a collapsible cane to support my slightly less stable walking, and for the first time, allowed myself to be transported by wheelchair through the chaotic Roman airport. It was worth it. *Here comes another one of Liesel's travelogues*, you might think, and you are right. I cannot help but rave about the mosaics in the Norman Monreale Cathedral, built between 1170–1189 outside of the city of Palermo. I would also recommend climbing the steep hill in Erice, where my walking stick came in handy. Halfway up the hill toward the local castle, we stopped to taste the amazing local pastries. To my surprise, when I reached the top and the magnificent view, a Santa Cruz golfing friend and her husband called out my name! The Overseas Adventure Travel company also made it possible for us to engage in a rare conversation with the son of a jailed Mafioso, giving us the opportunity to understand how difficult life is for a young man who does not share the mores of his elders but remains tied to them by loyalty and love of family.

After gazing at Roman ruins and visiting the charming tourist town of Taormina, we drove to the final stop on our tour and my world travels, Mount Etna, which just a month before our arrival had covered acres of land with a new layer of lava. Our local guide appear-

Liesel's donkey ride

ed, accompanied by donkeys, and with the guide's assistance, I mounted one to have another new experience. The guide's mother, in the

Singing Sicilian hostess

town just below the end of the lava flow, had prepared a typical Sicilian farewell dinner for us. As dessert was served, she proved that she was not only a great cook but a delightful entertainer. She jumped on a table and enthusiastically led us in songs from all over the world—a fitting and timely finale for this eighty-eight-year-old's world travels.

Sometime during that year, after returning home, I became an artist's model. My delightful neighbor and friend Jenny, a renowned portrait artist, is so highly regarded that the Portrait Society of America had requested her to paint a portrait of someone at its yearly gathering—in three hours!—so others could observe her in action. Jenny usually meets with her subjects, most of whom live on the East Coast, and after taking a multitude of photographs, returns home to paint an artistic rendition of what she saw. To practice for the upcoming event, I became her three-hour subject. I sat on my living room couch dressed in my favorite blouse, wearing the ring that is a copy of a 4,000-year-old Mesopotamian design from the Louvre and the Jensen watch acquired with unspent traveler cheques in Jerusalem. I also held a pillow I had embroidered on a canvas purchased in Chartres, France.

We met on three Wednesdays for an hour. The first hour she brought no paints but kept pointing a pencil at me and made a sketch. When she returned, she brought no sketch but came with a clean canvas and paints.

Phil & Jenny Welty

Stunned, I asked her what that first session had been about. She responded, "You're in my head now," and promptly painted the entire scene without my features, which she added during the third session. When Jenny entered the painting in the Portrait Society's annual competition, "Liesel" was among the best forty paintings of 1,800 that year. It now hangs in my living room, on a wall that is never in view when people are conversing. One Liesel in the room is enough.

Jenny Welty is much more than a portrait painter. She is the matriarch of a beautiful, large, cohesive evangelical family that I joined by becoming the "recently adopted great-grandmother" to baby Eden, the child of her eldest daughter, Taylor. This devout family loves Israel and all Jewish traditions because their Savior

was a Jew. I know they like me, yet the fact that I am Jewish makes me even more interesting. They now light Chanukah candles on a menorah I gave them, have a *mezuzah* on the doorpost of their home, and celebrate Passover as churches do these days—usually led by a Jew for Jesus, the latest denomination among religions, registered in the 1970s.

Liesel & Eden, 2022

I present one problem to that family; I cannot believe in a deity. Both Jenny and Taylor, diplomatically and with many references to their interpretations of the Bible, have gently but persistently tried to make me see the error of my ways. They predict that when the Rapture occurs, it will take all believers up to the Lord leaving nonbelievers like me behind, and that is unacceptable to them.

The patriarch of the Welty family is tall, handsome Phil, to whom I must now look up as I have shrunk 3.5 inches. Phil and his wife are both committed to doing whatever they can to help me continue to live in my home. He rolls my garbage cans up the steep incline I live on and appears with all kinds of tools to repair what is worn out or damaged. He plugs in his starter when I forget to turn off the lights in my car. He would like nothing better than for me to get back on the golf course to play the game we both love. Since that is now unlikely, I often join him in their cozy home to cheer our favorite golfers in major tournaments.

Time seems to pass so much faster as one ages, and therefore it was no great surprise when celebrations began for my ninetieth birthday on November 13, 2016. I had no lingering doubts that

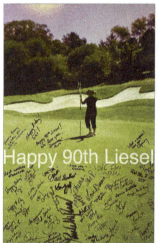
Signed poster from fellow golfers

the Jewish Liesel had become an integral part of the Pasatiempo Ladies' Golf Club, but I was overcome by the elaborate preparations for a special tournament in my honor. I rode in a decorated cart and played a hole with each player, who had been supplied with a ball marker with my picture. This was followed by a delicious luncheon at the beautiful home of my dear friend Sandi Selvi, whom we would lose to cancer much too early. Fifty or more people joined us at tables on the terrace around the pool. Everyone wore a scarf in my honor because I do not leave home without one (to cover the little hump on my neck).

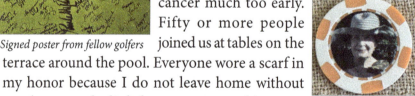
Birthday ball marker

Following my maternal ancestors' 150-year tradition of writing simple verses for friend and family celebrations, I wrote the following for that ninetieth birthday luncheon.

My Ninetieth

My almost 90 years have been blessed
Born in Germany, who would have guessed
That because I was born to parents who were wise
We left that country before Hitler's rise
For Holland and then to Canada in '39
Where our lives continued, and all was sublime

At 20 I met the intelligent charming Ernie
Together we started our 50-year journey
Lynn, Nancy and Daniel appeared on the scene
Life in Montreal was wonderfully serene
Until separatism reared its ugly head
A movement that we all did dread

What should we do, where should we go?
We certainly no longer wished to live in the snow
So, after five years of waiting for permission
The US finally made the right decision
And allowed us to live in what Ernie called paradise
I guess just like my parents we too were wise

Sadly, this fine man was assailed
By Alzheimer's, his life was curtailed
After 17 beautiful years in paradise
I, now widowed, had to become more wise

I was unreasonably beset by fears
But decided not to break out in tears
A five-year contract with myself I made
To live fully and not be afraid

This contract, now renewed on 4 occasions
Has been nourished by my relations
With you and many others not present today
In my recollections they will always stay

During 32 years in this wonderful place
Memories were created that I shall not erase

Pasatiempo, new friends, volunteering, being involved
Around this my life in Santa Cruz has revolved

In 1983 I joined our beautiful club
I had to qualify to be able tee up
More ladies played in those years
With a twelve on 16 I qualified despite tears

The first few years as an 18-holer
I carried my bag, yes I did, upon my shoulder
Then pushed a canvas cart like our friend Betty
About 15 years ago I was good and ready
For Pat Hamilton's recommendation, the electronic caddy
Now in my older years I have needed it badly

The ladies now suggest "Liesel, take a cart"
So that my slower pace will not retard
The fast-moving game that is now demanded
You're behind, please split up and run like a bandit

We, the 18-hole group, thrive on competition
That's right up my alley so I made a decision
To lower one's handicap was the name of the game
That can be demanding and now is a great strain

The Neuf Trous ladies are a splendid bunch
They play noncompetitive golf and relax over lunch
Socialize frequently at specific functions
Their numbers are increasing at every junction

Statistics, I hear, can evaluate success
If I were to attempt this subject it would be a mess
Logging the hours we shared on our beautiful links
Would be a staggering concept, methinks

I have worked with most of you for the good of our club
Your camaraderie and efficiency were over the top
Thank you much for your friendship and this celebration
Here's to holes-in-one and chip-ins on many occasions.

The birthday celebration continued when another neighbor and bridge partner, Harold Rogers, opened his spacious home to host a party for as many friends as I wanted to invite. Mimi Stein and Yelena Kratz, the official Liesel Sabloff birthday coordinators since my eightieth birthday, collaborated with him in his private domain—his kitchen—to produce the fabulous food, including the special birthday cake Hal baked himself. I believe that more than fifty people attended that joyful event, including my two younger children, Nancy and Daniel, who flew in for the occasion. We missed Lynn greatly but did not want her to risk

Mimi & Elena

flying because her immune system was compromised. I did, however, receive a beautiful, loving letter from my eldest daughter, which turned out to be the last communication I would ever receive from her.

Just four days into 2016, I received a phone call from one of Lynn's friends in the Dominican Republic gently telling me that my daughter was missing and had not been heard from for several days. I believe that any parent receiving this news can identify with my anxiety and fear, although I was assured by a Canadian police officer (who happened to be in Cabrera to improve the shoddy policing in that country) that he was doing everything in his power to find my daughter. But he and Lynn's friends also informed me that two other people had been killed in Cabrera during the days that Lynn was first missing, and that their murderers, who had been imprisoned and released before their sentences were served, had been identified. These same men had been seen driving Lynn's car down the remote road where she lived.

Four days after receiving this unbelievable news, my children and I had little hope left, but it took another week for us to learn that an unrecognizable body had washed ashore in a remote cove of the Atlantic that was presumed to be the remains of my beautiful Lynn.

I have always considered myself strong enough to be able to cope with adversity, but this tragedy overwhelmed me. There was nothing I could do or could have done to change what had happened and I felt useless. Why Nancy suggested, "Mom, go clean the house," I will never know. But I did just that and, to my surprise, found that the act of accomplishing something gave me a feeling of satisfaction and purpose that I completely lacked in dealing with Lynn's murder. It turns out that this is exactly what Hospice would have suggested to a person in my condition.

Lynn's friend informed us that a lawyer she knew, Marta, a social activist in Cabrera, was ready to take on our case. Three of us, the astute Yelena Kraz, Nancy and I, spoke with her on the phone. She sounded kind and empathetic and asked us to put our trust in her to resolve legal and personal matters in this tragedy. When we inquired what her hourly fee would be, she gave the three of us the impression that she was offering her services out of the goodness of her heart. When we repeated that question on numerous occasions during the next months, we always got the same answer.

Without DNA identification, we could not lay Lynn to rest, get access to her bank account in Cabrera, or sell her property. We hired a property manager to keep her house, garden, and pool in proper order. Eventually we got permission to rent the property, but that proved to be difficult because of the history it now had. During the first year, the Dominican lab that was to match Lynn's DNA test to my own put all kinds of barriers in our way. No authority could help, not the Canadian Embassy nor the Dominican government. We were stymied at every turn. Marta was upset when I refused to finance the trials of the two perpetrators. I believed that the country's prosecutors should be paid by their own government, the same people who had given these criminals their freedom when they should have remained in jail.

I cannot recall how Marta was able to find out how much money was in Lynn's bank account, but about a year and a half into this process, we received an outrageous contract from her in which she demanded to be paid one-third of all Lynn's assets, which would have made her an heir, with Daniel and Nancy, to Lynn's estate. Marta was paid for her meager accomplishments; we dismissed her and hired the highly regarded firm of Ariza Guzman, whom Lynn had used to buy her property.

With their help and connections, my daughter's life was eventually brought to closure. It took close to three years of these hurdles to receive DNA confirmation that the remains were Lynn's. The local bank released her funds, and our daughter was finally laid to rest.

Several of Lynn's friends wondered why no one from our family flew to the D.R. to engage in the legal proceedings and be present when the house was emptied of her belongings. There was no way that I would return to that lawless country, nor did I want either of my two remaining children to set foot there unless it was essential. Lynn's house was simply furnished; she had only three items she treasured that *Lynn Sabloff by J. Welty* were of comparatively little value, and we felt that we did not have to be present to dissolve her household. A Canadian friend of hers accompanied the realtor who managed the house to look for her topaz ring, a painting by a Canadian artist, and the little Egyptian amulet of Horace that had come from Captain Churchill's collection in the big box we had opened on the stairs of our house in Montreal when she was ten. Even then, she had wanted nothing more than to own it, but neither it nor the ring were to be found.

Her friends in Cabrera held a memorial in the home she had built and loved. I have a little corner in the room where I am writing that is filled with pictures of Lynn, surrounding a striking 10 x 14-inch sketch by Jennifer Welty that she presented to me a week after Lynn's death. Tears always fall when I think or write about this tragedy, but like so many other parents, I have been able to march on and learn to live with having so painfully lost my daughter.

During the summer of 2016, while we were trying to solve our problems in the Dominican Republic, I contracted campylobacter, a bacterium that causes severe diarrhea, for which I was prescribed two extraordinarily strong medications that I was to take for a full ten days. After three days, although the diarrhea had subsided, Nancy (who was visiting at time) and I became extremely concerned because the medicine did not allow me to sleep a wink, I had no appetite, and my otherwise perfectly good vision was impaired. A second doctor told me that this medication is usually prescribed for only one or two days until the symptoms are gone, and not to take any more. I was genuinely concerned that an overdose might have affected my otherwise healthy system.

I slowly recovered my good health, but that October my legs began to feel different. I was standing outside the body shop where my car was being repaired when my left leg felt like it did not want to move. Had those pills caused the neuropathy that now affected my legs? Would my otherwise healthy body be forced to use a wheelchair and never be able to play another round of golf? I will not enumerate all the medical procedures we attempted to cure my problem or relieve the severity of what I experienced during the next four years, some of which were helpful but none of which corrected the problem entirely. However, as time passed, I became accustomed to my limitation.

The good news is that, even now at age ninety-six, I do not use a wheelchair or a walker. Although I am happy to have a shopping cart to hold onto, I still make my way around the grocery store and navigate quite well on even ground, only needing my walking poles or a supportive arm on uneven territory. I still drive. I treasure the fact that I can live alone and am able to clean my house superficially and cook for myself. I firmly believe that this is only possible because I continue to exercise daily, walk for fifteen minutes with twopound weights every afternoon, and have the good fortune to socialize frequently with the people I call friends.

One of these friends is Barbara Black, whom we call "the gatherer" because it gives her such pleasure to bring people together.

One day in September of 2016, she took me aside with an offer I knew was to help distract me from my loss. "Liesel, I can get very reasonable airline tickets to New York at this time. I have been invited to stay in a penthouse with a good friend and am planning to go to a musical and some museums. Take your time to think whether you want to join me." I needed no time to think and responded enthusiastically that I would love to join her.

My suitcase came out of retirement for yet another trip, during which we stayed with her delightful friend and visited the Neue Galerie's Gustav Klimt exhibit, which included *The Woman in Gold*. This painting was stolen from a prominent Austrian Jewish family by Nazis, and its story was made into a movie by the same name. We attended a musical, and Barbara saw to it that we got tickets for my first visit to Carnegie

Barbara Black & Liesel

Hall to hear a concert with my favorite conductor, Gustavo Dudamel, leading the famous young musicians from his native Venezuela. Most importantly, we toured the museum of the 9/11 tragedy and admired the architecture of the dramatic new white-winged subway station, the Oculus, built on that site. The afternoon of the fifth day, we decided we had to walk across

The Oculus

the famous Brooklyn Bridge before going our separate ways to visit friends for a few days and then flying home together.

I traveled to Deal, New Jersey, where my young Israeli friend Miriam, with whom I had attended a media course in Montreal, now lived with her husband Ralph. Ralph's family had escaped from Aleppo, Syria in the early part of the twentieth century. Deal is the summer retreat for Syrian Jewish descendants who reside in

Brooklyn and who hope that their children will become acquainted with like-minded mates during those months.

It was my good fortune that Miriam's mother, whom I had met before, was visiting from Israel. This Holocaust survivor lived with her family in Poland and entered Auschwitz at the age of fourteen. She survived only because her mother had the opportunity to take her daughter with her when she was sent to a labor camp, two weeks after entering the concentration camp. Her father and her brother did not survive. This intelligent and attractive lady moved to Israel after she married, raised three daughters and had nine grandchildren—but her experiences during the Holocaust were never far from her mind.

Miriam had taught Hebrew at a Jewish day school in Deal for numerous years. She had asked me to pack the folder with my grandmother's information to share with her tenth-grade students while I told the story. To my surprise, these students showed a keen interest in my story and were most impressed by the picture of me looking at my grandmother's suitcase from outside as well as inside the glass wall at the museum in Auschwitz. Miriam and I still laugh about the fact that the fashion-minded girls in her class complimented my tightly laced black Bernie Mev sandals with their 2.5-inch wedge heels that make me almost as tall as I once was. Little did they know that their compliments made me very happy because, since 2016, those are the only shoes that I own that are attractive and narrow enough to let me walk in comfort. I have worn out several pairs but always have an extra in my closet.

2016 was also the year we watched the presidential debates between Hillary Clinton and Donald Trump. Like many of my contemporaries, I was stunned when this New York businessperson and reality TV star won the election and, although throughout this entire story I have not dwelt on the politics of this great nation, the Trump presidency disturbed me too greatly not to mention it. It was frightening to listen to his numerous town halls where the audiences showed no restraint to hoot and holler when this undisciplined leader sang his own praises and denigrated opponents.

The fact that governing this nation became a family affair, like the businesses he had been engaged in, was also highly unusual. He had no tolerance for any member of his cabinet or party who disagreed with him, and Republican party leaders followed his doctrinaire leadership without question. Even today, in 2022, most Republicans are unable to sever themselves from him, although he has gone as far as to mesmerize a radical group of mostly white supremacists who attacked the Capitol Building when he lost the election to Joe Biden the following year. It is so sad that this fierce loyalty to party has divided the nation along political lines that even families and friends of different political stripes do not dare to cross, and which has prevented people from listening to each other's opinions and arriving at a consensus for the good of all.

President Biden moved into the White House in 2021 and wanted to unite this nation. He ensured that all its citizens were vaccinated (when vaccines were available) and proposed an agenda that he hoped would pass both houses of the government and reestablish the American commitment to our NATO allies that President Trump had severed. But even those who believe in vaccination against COVID-19 are at odds with the unvaccinated and vice versa, creating controversies that sadly have resulted in permanent breakage of longtime friendships of people I know.

Still, hope springs eternal. Mine is that this great nation's democracy will survive and that people of different political parties, religions, shades of skin or ethnicity will be regarded as full and equal citizens. So much more can be achieved with human kindness and dignity.

In October of 2019, my oldest longtime friend, Bernie Issenman, passed away at age ninety-eight in his home in Santa Cruz. During *shiva*, Bernie was remembered as the adoring husband of Ruth, the loving father of four, proud grandfather of seven, and great-grandfather of five. He was a highly respected and accomplished businessman and was loyal to anyone he called friend.

At his shiva, Greg Morris, Bernie's oldest grandson-in-law, took me aside and insisted, not for the first time, "Liesel, you have to write your story." My response to Greg and others who thought that to be a good idea has always been, "Every person's life is a story. What makes mine any more interesting than another's?"

But as I looked around that room I was struck, not for the first time, by how adaptive we human beings are—and that is enough reason to sit down and record our history. Here I was surrounded by the offspring of Ruth, the daughter of Orthodox Jews who fled to Canada from Romania, and Bernie, the son of Russian Jews who also sought a haven in that country. Their ancestors would have been stunned to observe that their grandchildren had intermarried with different faiths and that seven of their great-grandchildren have gentile mates. Like Tevye in *Fiddler on the Roof*, they would have exclaimed "Unheard of! Unthinkable!" Unlike Tevye, Ruth and Bernie not only adapted but also welcomed everyone into their close-knit family, and they were happy that some are raising Jewish children in countries where this is possible.

Four months after Bernie's shiva, as COVID-19 spread and affected the lives of everyone on the planet, I was told that because of my age I was quite vulnerable to becoming infected. At that point, I felt that I'd been granted longevity just to experience more of the world's disasters. But I was also inspired to sit down and start writing, as most other activities were curtailed.

Bridge Club, Liesel at right of table

During the pandemic, when our bridge club was closed, I joined my partners to play online on a website called BBO, where sometimes more than 30,000 people are registered at the same time and (as we are invisible) our appearance is of no consequence. I have now returned to play some games at the club in the presence of friends, for whom I don my finery, but I do love to play in my housecoat a few times a week.

In August 2020, fires were raging in the Santa Cruz Mountains and I was told that I should evacuate immediately. Very worried and afraid, I packed my car with important papers, clothing for all seasons, most of the remaining artwork that I treasure, and those important sandals, and was safely installed in the comfortable Kraz home to wait out the threat. Thankfully, ten days later I was given a green light to return home.

I know that a great deal of brutality is inflicted on many people on our planet, but I never considered that I would live long enough to watch another dictator of a developed nation launch an unprovoked attack on a neighboring country, destroying its infrastructure, murdering thousands, and leaving millions homeless so he can take possession of a land he deems his to take. Vladimir Putin's reasons for committing these horrible crimes in Ukraine are different from Adolf Hitler's, but neither had regard for their fellow human beings. This Russian criminal should be put behind bars for life and all the wealth he and his oligarchs have amassed should be used to rebuild what he has destroyed.

So say I, but that verdict is unlikely to be considered.

In the twentieth century, children from Germany, Poland, the Czech Republic, Hungary, Syria, and other nations attacked by powerful enemies were uprooted from family and friends and forced to leave their homes, in most cases with just a suitcase and the hope that they would be welcomed by peaceful, neighboring nations. Now it is Ukraine. Most of their stories may never be heard. This little Jewish girl from Chemnitz who escaped during the Holocaust was luckier than most displaced children. I was able to lead a full and interesting life because my family was admitted, although with difficulty, into Canada and the US, two beautiful nations that share an exceedingly long, peaceful border. It has been my good fortune never to experience overt anti-Semitism, yet I know that despite isolated incidents even on this continent, an undercurrent exists that can be awakened in challenging times, when a scapegoat is needed. That is why we Jews must never forget, nor allow the world to forget, what happened during the Holocaust.

If all humankind—no matter what race, religion, or nationality—would commit themselves to following the precept, "Do unto your neighbor as you would do unto yourself," we would be living in a far more peaceful world where stories of war and destruction need not be written.

Before I leave you to ponder this utopian ideal, I want to tell you how grateful I am to have lived long enough to be able to complete this story. Fortunately, I am well enough at ninety-six-and-a-half—yes, that is how I now calculate my age—and if things continue as they are at present, I will be ninety-six-and-three-quarters in August of 2022, marching about with hearing aids in my ears, an alarm button around my neck, in my comfortable black sandals, with my walking stick at hand.

I will be living, as I am, a full life for a little longer.

Mark Kraz sat me down at his drums in 2021, and that just may become my next hobby, now that my writing is done.

Above: Josef Frank
Below: Margaret Frank
nee Herrmann

Frank Brothers
- Otto
- Josef —
  married

Herrmann Siblings
- Margaret
- Harry m. Rosel
- Theo m. Elsa
- Willi m. Claire
- Max

My Mother's Family

Lotte m. Arthur Becker ──┐ Fritz
                             Ziesel* m. Ernie Sabloff

Rudi m. Herta

Kurt (the Ritchie Boy) m. Sue Grosz ── Robert

Erna •─── Edith (Sent to Scotland on the "Kinder Transport")

Walter •

Fritz — Moved to Johannesburg and created a large extended family

Escaped to Columbia with entire family

── Died Young

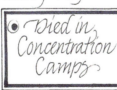

• Died in Concentration Camps

Acknowledgements

FOR SOMEONE WHO wrote poor compositions in school and never grasped the grammar lessons in English or any other language, what did I think I was doing? Telling a story is so very different from writing on a computer—where it seemed that it suddenly could not be found, or the editing possibilities disappeared because I hit a wrong key, and either Vladimir Kraz or another good friend, like bridge and computer guru Ken Llacera, had to come to the rescue.

However, I kept hitting those keys on my keyboard and produced a body of writing that caused my honest niece Carla, who read it, to suggest that I hire an editor, which I did. For almost two years the competent, caring Betty Marton, now my good friend, has encouraged me to keep on writing and even claimed that I am a much better writer than I think I am—of which you are now the judge.

It seems as if I have been reliving my entire life in the past two years. Often, when I tried to recall my past, I would dream strange dreams and get up in the middle of the night to scribble down a fact that I thought could or should be inserted into what I had written during the day. You might consider yourself fortunate that I did not record all my nightly musings. I consider myself fortunate to have been granted some extra time to see this writing published.

I am grateful for all the assistance I received from valuable people. My neighbor, Jenny Welty, offered to digitize a multitude of pictures, some of which were inserted in this book. Another neighbor, the accomplished calligrapher Ruth Korch, created the complicated artistic family tree to help the reader sort out all my family relations. My capable, experienced copyeditor, Melody

Culver, stepped into action and with unending patience placed the pictures in the most appropriate places. She and Casey Coonerty, a granddaughter of the Issenmans whom I have known and admired since she was born and who is now the owner of Bookshop Santa Cruz, saw to it that this story was published.

As I express my sincere thanks to these four accomplished women, I also want to acknowledge Ruth Miller, my Toronto cousin (a writer herself), who read every chapter as it was edited and kept encouraging me to keep writing.

All of you who have touched my life in any way are part of this story as well, even if your name is not mentioned in this book.

The kaleidoscope of all whom I have met is who I have become.